THE BOY FROM THE RANCH

Or, Roy Bradner's City Experiences

FRANK V. WEBSTER

1st WORLD
LIBRARY
Literary Society

The Boy from the Ranch

Frank V. Webster

© 1st World Library, 2007
PO Box 2211
Fairfield, IA 52556
www.1stworldlibrary.com
First Edition

LCCN: 2007934119

Softcover ISBN: 978-1-4218-9642-7
Hardcover ISBN: 978-1-4218-9742-4
eBook ISBN: 978-1-4218-9542-0

Purchase *"The Boy from the Ranch"*
as a traditional bound book at:
www.1stWorldLibrary.com/purchase.asp?ISBN=978-1-4218-9642-7

1st World Library is a literary, educational organization
dedicated to:

- Creating a free internet library of downloadable ebooks

- Hosting writing competitions and offering book publishing
scholarships.

Interested in more 1st World Library books? contact:
literacy@1stworldlibrary.com
Check us out at: www.1stworldlibrary.com

1ˢᵗ World Library Literary Society

Giving Back to the World

"If you want to work on the core problem, it's early school literacy."

- James Barksdale, former CEO of Netscape

"No skill is more crucial to the future of a child, or to a democratic and prosperous society, than literacy."

- Los Angeles Times

"Literacy... means far more than learning how to read and write... The aim is to transmit... knowledge and promote social participation."

- UNESCO

"Literacy is not a luxury, it is a right and a responsibility. If our world is to meet the challenges of the twenty-first century we must harness the energy and creativity of all our citizens."

- President Bill Clinton

"Parents should be encouraged to read to their children, and teachers should be equipped with all available techniques for teaching literacy, so the varying needs and capacities of individual kids can be taken into account."

- Hugh Mackay

CONTENTS

CHAPTER I

ROY RECEIVES A MESSAGE

"Hi there, Low Bull, ruste [Transcriber's note: rustle?] around the other way and round up them steers! Hustle now! What's the matter with you? Want to go to sleep on the trail?"

Billy Carew, foreman of the Triple O ranch, addressed these remarks to a rather ugly-looking Indian, who was riding a pony that seemed much too small for him. The Indian, who was employed as a cowboy, was letting his steed amble slowly along, paying little attention to the work of rounding up the cattle.

"Come now, Low Bull, get a move on," advised the foreman. "Make believe you're hunting palefaces," he added, and then, speaking in a lower tone he said: "this is the last time I'll ever hire a lazy Indian to help round-up."

"What's the matter, Billy?" asked a tall, well-built lad, riding up to the foreman.

"Matter? Everything's the matter. Here I foolishly go and give Low Bull charge of the left wing of rounding up these steers, and he's so lazy and good-for-nothing that he'll let half of 'em get away 'fore we get back to the ranch. Get a move on you now!" he called to the Indian, and, seeing that the foreman was very much in earnest, Low Bull urged his pony to a gallop, and began to get the straggling steers into some kind of shape.

"Can't I help you, Billy?" asked the boy.

Since he is to figure largely in this story I shall give you a brief description of him. Roy Bradner was the only son of James Bradner, who owned a large ranch, near the town of Painted Stone, in Colorado. The boy's mother was dead, and he had lived with his father on the ranch ever since he was a baby.

Spending much of his time in the open air, Roy had become almost as strong and sturdy as a man, and in some respects he could do the work of one.

He was quite expert in managing horses, even steeds that had never known a saddle, and at throwing the lariat, or lasso, few on the ranch could beat him. He was a good shot with the revolver and rifle, and, in short, was a typical western boy.

"Can't I help you, Billy?" the lad asked again, as he saw the foreman had not appeared to hear his question.

"Yes, I wish you would, Roy. Ride up there alongside of Low Bull, and sort of keep him up to the mark. It sure looks as if he was going to sleep in the saddle."

"I'll do it, Billy. Where are we going to camp to-night?"

"Well, I guess if we make a few miles more I'll call it a day's work and quit. We've done pretty well, and if Low Bull would have done his share, we'd be nearer the ranch than we are now. I don't want any better round-up men than Nesting Henderson and the rest, but we need another man, and that's why I had to take Low Bull along. But I'll know better next time."

"Never mind, Billy. I'll see if I can't keep him on the go," said Roy, and, with a ringing shout, to hurry up some lagging steers, he touched his horse lightly with the spurs, and dashed toward where the Indian was making a half-hearted effort to keep his division of the drive from straggling.

"I've come to help you, Low Bull," announced Roy, as he reached the side of the Indian.

"Hu! Boy heap smart!" grunted the redman. "Steers like boy—go fast now."

In fact it seemed as if the cattle knew some one was now behind them who would keep them on the move, for they quickened their pace.

"I don't know whether they like me or not," remarked Roy, with a laugh that showed his white teeth in contrast to his bronzed skin, "for I reckon if I happened to fall off my horse they'd trample over me mighty quick; they sure would."

"Hu! Mebby so. Steers no like men not on hoss," spoke Low Bull, stating a fact well known among cattlemen, for the steers of the plains are so used to seeing a man on a horse, that once a cowboy is dismounted the cattle become frightened, and are liable to stampede, and trample the unfortunate man to death.

"Billy says we must hurry the steers along," went on Roy. "We're going to camp pretty soon, and he wants to get to the ranch as soon as possible, though I guess it will take us two days more."

"No need so much rush," said Low Bull. "Go slow be better. Boy drive steers now, Low Bull take smoke and think. Low Bull much tired."

"I guess he was born that way," thought Roy, as he saw the redman start to make a cigarette, a habit he had learned from the white cowboys. Low Bull was soon smoking in peace and comfort, while he let his pony amble along at its own sweet will. The Indian gave no further thought to the cattle, leaving the management of the stragglers to Roy, and the lad had to dash here and there on his nimble pony, shouting and waving his lariat, to keep the lagging steers up with the rest of the herd. However, Roy was so full of life, and took so much interest in his work, that he did not mind doing Low Bull's share, as well as his own.

"That's just like that lazy Indian," remarked Billy Carew, as he observed, from a distance, what Roy was doing. "He'll let the boy do all the work. I'll discharge him after this round-up, that's what I'll do. Might have known better than to hire one of them copper-skins!"

Roy, whose father owned the Triple O ranch, had come out on this round-up about a week previously. On all big ranches it is the custom, at stated intervals to send out a party of men to round-up, or gather together, in herds, the cattle or horses that may have strayed to distant pastures.

Sometimes a week or more is spent on this work, the men sleeping out of doors, and making camp wherever darkness overtakes them. During the night they take turns riding around the cattle, to keep them from straying away.

Day by day the herd is driven nearer the ranch, until they are

Frank V. Webster

either placed in corrals, which are big pens, or are counted, brands put on the new calves, and turned out again, to roam about over the immense pastures, and fatten up for the market.

Mr. Bradner was an extensive ranch owner, and had several herds of cattle. He was considered quite wealthy, but he had made his money by hard work, having very little when he first went out west with his wife and little boy. His wife had died soon after he reached Colorado, and, after his baby days, Roy had been brought up by his father.

The boy liked the life on the ranch, and was fast becoming an expert along cattle lines. He was a good judge of steers and horses, and, while he knew nothing of city ways, never since a mere infant having been in anything larger than a town, and not having traveled more than a few miles, there was nothing about life on the plains but what he was acquainted with.

After much hard riding Roy managed to get that part of the herd entrusted to the Indian, into compact form. Then he came back to his companion, who was riding along as if he had nothing more to think about than keeping his cigarette lighted.

"Hu! Heap smart boy!" grunted Low Bull. "Know how make steers travel."

"I should think you would know how to do it too," said Roy. "You've always lived on the plains."

"Too much work. Indian no like work. Like sit an' think, an' smoke. No like work."

"Everybody's got to work in this world, Low Bull."

"Rich man no work. Me like be rich man."

"But the man sure had to work hard to get rich. I s'pose rich men feel that they can take life easy after they have earned a fortune."

"Indian no like work. Drive cattle too hard. Me quit soon," was all Low Bull replied.

"Yes, and if you don't quit I think Billy will make you vamoose anyhow," murmured Roy.

Low Bull rolled another cigarette, and seemed to go to sleep under the influence of it. Roy had to race off after a couple of straying steers, and had no further time for talking. When he had brought the cattle back, a long, shrill cry echoed over the plain. At the sound of it Low Bull seemed to wake up.

"Billy make camp now," he said. "Soon supper—eat—Low Bull hungry."

It was the signal for making camp, and, finding themselves no longer urged forward, the steers stopped, and began to crop the rich grass.

The cowboys, of whom there were several, with joyful shouts, came riding up to the cook wagon, which had been pulled along in the rear, but which now came to a halt on the broad, rolling plain. "Smoke" Tardell started a fire from grease-wood, and began to prepare the evening meal.

"Set out plenty of grub, Smoke," called one of the cowboys, riding close up to Tardell, and playfully snatching his big sombrero off.

"Here! You let that be, Bruce Arkdell!" exclaimed the cook.

"That's my new hat, an' I don't want it spoiled!"

"Give me an extra plate of beans, or I'll shoot a hole in it!" threatened the cowboy, drawing hit heavy revolver, and aiming it at the hat, which he held in one hand.

"All right. You can have three platesful, but don't you spoil my hat!" cried the cook, as he received back his sombrero. "I never see such crazy chaps as them boys be when they're headed for the ranch," muttered "Smoke," as he set the coffee pot over the fire.

It did not take long to prepare the meal, and the cowboys crowded around the "grub wagon" as they called it. Low Bull was among them, his eyes greedy for food.

"Here, Low Bull," exclaimed Billy Carew, "you go out and ride around them steers awhile. They ain't quieted down yet, and I don't want no stampede now. Ride around 'em, and make 'em feel easy."

"After supper," said the Indian.

"No, now!" insisted the foreman.

"Low Bull hungry. Like eat."

"Low Bull is going to stay hungry then, until some of the others have piled in their grub," declared Billy. "I'll send somebody out to take your place, as soon as they've eaten. Now vamoose!"

"Low Bull like eat."

"Yes, I know. Low Bull like eat, but no like work. That's what's the matter with Low Bull," exclaimed Billy with a laugh. "Now git."

The Indian knew there was no use disputing this decision, so, with no very good grace, he started to ride slowly around the cattle, to keep them from moving off in a body.

"I'll go out and relieve him in a little while," offered Roy. "I'll soon be through supper."

"You take your time now, son," advised Billy. "It won't hurt that redskin to go hungry a while. Maybe he'll be a little sprier after this."

Supper was soon served, and when Roy had eaten his share he prepared to go out, and relieve Low Bull. He threw the saddle over his pony's back, and, having tightened the girths, was about to vault into place, when he and the other cowboys became aware that some one was riding in great haste toward the temporary camp.

"Somebody's coming," remarked Bruce Arkdell.

"Don't you s'pose we know it," said Billy good naturedly. "We've got our sight yet."

"Yes, and it's Porter Simms, from the way he gallops," added the cook, shading his eyes from the setting sun, and peering across the prairies at the riding man.

"'Tis Porter," confirmed Billy. "Wonder what he wants? Hope nothing's happened."

Somehow the words sent a slight feeling of fear to Roy's heart. The man might have bad news for some one in camp.

"Is Roy here?" cried Porter, as soon as he had come within

talking distance.

"Yes, I'm here," replied the boy. "What's the matter? Is it my father—?"

"Now don't go gettin' skeered," advised Porter, as he pulled up his horse sharply. "I sure did ride fast to locate you, but your daddy wanted me to be sure to tell you, first-off, not to git skeered."

"What's the matter?" asked Roy, his heart fluttering.

"Well, your daddy's a little under the weather, and he wants for you to come back to the ranch right away. That's the message I was to give to you. Don't wait to come in with the steers, but start right off. I'll stay here and take your place."

"Is he—was he very bad?" asked Roy, who had left his father, seemingly, in perfect health.

"No, not so very I guess. The doctor was there, and he didn't seem much put out. I reckon Mr. Bradner had a sort of a bad turn, that's all."

"I'll start right away," decided Roy. "If I ride all night I can get there by morning."

"Don't you want one of us to go with you?" asked Billy.

"No. I'm not afraid. I've done it before. Smoke, will you pack me a little grub?"

"Surest thing you know!" exclaimed the cook, as he began to do up some bacon and bread.

CHAPTER II

MR. BRADNER IS SUSPICIOUS

Crowding around Roy in ready sympathy, the cowboys questioned Porter as to the state of affairs at the ranch. The messenger knew very little about it. He had been to a distant pasture land, when he had been summoned to the ranch house by another cowboy, who was sent after him. When he got back he found Mr. Bradner quite ill.

"He said he wanted me to go for Roy," went on Porter, "'cause he knew I could ride fast. But he particular didn't want Roy to git worried. He said it was as much a business matter as anything."

"Maybe he's goin' to die an' wants to make his will," suggested one of the cowboys.

"Here! What's the matter with you! Don't you know no better than that?" demanded Billy in a hoarse whisper. "Want to give Roy a scare? I'll peg you out if you do that again!"

"I—I didn't think!"

"No, I guess you didn't. Lucky he didn't hear you. Now you think twice before you speak once, after this."

Frank V. Webster

"Here's your grub," announced the cook, holding out a big package to Roy. It contained enough food for three men, but Roy was a favorite with "Smoke," as indeed he was with all the men on the ranch, and this was the only way the genius of the camp-fire could show his affection.

"Say, what do you think he goin' to do? Be three days on the home trail?" asked Billy. "He don't want no snack like that. He can't carry it."

"I thought maybe he'd be hungry in the night."

"I expect I will be, but not enough to get away with all that," remarked Roy with a smile, as he saw the big package. "I just want a little bread, and some cold bacon."

The cook, with a sigh at the thought of the boy not being able to eat all the food, made a smaller package. Meanwhile Roy was in the saddle, ready to travel, wondering what could be the matter with his father, and why his parent had sent for him in such a hurry.

"Got your gun?" asked Porter.

"Yes," answered Roy, tapping the pistol in its holster at his belt.

"Maybe you'd better take my pony," suggested Billy. "He can travel faster than yours."

"No; Jack Rabbit's good enough for me," replied the boy, patting his own pony on the neck. "Yours may be a bit faster, but Jack Rabbit will stick longer. Well, I'm off!"

"Good luck!" called Billy.

"Don't worry!" advised Porter.

"We'll see you in a couple of days," shouted the other cowboys. "Take care of yourself."

"I will," said Roy, as he called to his pony, who started off on a steady "lope" that rapidly carried him over the ground.

Now that he was away from the confusion of the camp, and had nothing to distract his mind, Roy gave himself up to thoughts of his father.

"He must be quite sick," he reasoned, "or he never would have sent for me in such a rush. I wonder if Porter was afraid to tell me the truth?"

For an instant the fear that his father might be dead, and that the cowboy had not dared to tell him of it, unnerved Roy. Then his natural braveness came back to him.

"Oh, pshaw! What's the use of thinking such gloomy thoughts," he said to himself. "Maybe dad only had a little fit of indigestion, like he had before. I remember then I thought he sure was going to die. But Porter said it was as much business as anything else. Now what sort of business could dad have that he would need me in such a hurry?"

Roy did not see any prospect of his questions being answered, at least until he got to the ranch, and could talk to his father, so he continued on, urging his pony to a faster gait.

It soon began to get dark, but Roy did not mind this, as he had often ridden all night when on a round-up. Of course, on such occasions he had been in company with his father's cowboys. Still, the prospect of his lonely journey through the

Frank V. Webster

darkness did not alarm him.

He knew the trail very well, from having been over it often, and, though there were occasionally ugly Indians, or unemployed cowboys, to be met with on the plains, Roy did not imagine he would have any trouble with them. He was armed, but he hoped he would have no occasion to draw his revolver.

There were no wild animals, except steers, to be met and these, he knew, would be in herds under the care of competent men. Besides a steer rarely attacks a man on a horse.

So Roy rode through the long night. About one o'clock he stopped, built a little grease-wood fire, and warmed his bacon. Then he munched that and the bread with a good appetite, drinking some coffee the cook had given him in a flask.

"I ought to get to the ranch by sun-up," thought the boy, and he was not mistaken, for, when the golden ball peeped up over the prairies Roy saw the outbuildings of his father's big cattle farm. A little later he had ridden up to the ranch house, and dismounted.

"My father! How is he?" he exclaimed, as he saw the cook on the verandah.

"Better," was the reply, and the boy felt a sense of relief. "Much better. Come right in and have some hot coffee. I've got it all ready for you."

"Not until I've seen my father," and Roy hurried into the ranch house.

"Is that you, Roy?" called a voice from a bedroom.

"Yes, father! How are you?"

"Considerable better. I hope you were not alarmed."

"Well, I was—some."

Roy saw that his father was in bed. The man looked quite pale, and on a stand, near him, were several bottles of medicine.

"What is it, father?" asked Roy. "What happened?"

"Well, nothing much, though I was afraid it was at the time. I got one of my bad spells of indigestion, and it affected my heart."

"Did you think you were going to die?"

"Well, I did, but the doctor only laughed at me. He said I was needlessly alarmed, and I think, now, that I was. But when I was in such pain, fearing something would happen, I thought of a business matter that needed attending to. I decided I had better get my affairs in shape—in case anything should happen, so I sent for you, to have a talk."

"What sort of a talk, father?"

"A business talk. I'm going to have you undertake something in an entirely new line. You're a pretty good cattleman now, and I want to see how you'll make out on a business deal."

"What kind?"

"I'll soon explain. But tell me; how is Billy, and the boys?"

"Very well."

"Are they getting the cattle in good shape? Where did Porter find you?"

"The cattle will be here to-morrow, I think. Porter came up just as we were camping out near the small dried creek in the big swale," replied Roy, describing the place so that his father would know it. "But now tell me about this business. I am glad you are better."

"Yes, I feel much improved. My indigestion is all gone, and I think I can eat breakfast. I'll tell you then."

Roy could hardly wait for the meal to be finished. After his father had had his repast in bed, Mr. Bradner told his son to close the door, and sit down close beside him.

"I'm going to take you into my confidence," said the ranch owner. "It's time you knew something of my business affairs, and I am going to entrust you with a commission. A good deal depends on the success of it."

"I hope I can do it, father."

"I am pretty sure you can, or I would not let you go. Now I'll tell you what it is. You do not know it, but I have an interest in some property, left by your mother's brother, your Uncle Henry Mayfield. This property was left to your mother, and when she died the property came to me, and to you. That is, I have a third interest in it, and you have two-thirds."

"That hardly seems fair. You should have more than I."

"Never mind, Roy. In fact I intend that, in time, you shall have the whole of the property."

"Where is it located?"

"In New York City."

"New York? That is a long way off."

"Yes, a good many miles. In fact I have never seen the property. It is in charge of an agent—a real estate man. Every month he sends me the money received for rent, and, for several years I have put your share away, at interest in a bank."

"Then I have some money saved up, and did not know it."

"That is right, and it is quite a sum. But, of late, the rents have been falling off, until they are only about half what they were when your mother owned the property."

"Why is this?"

"The agent says it is because the property has gone down in value, but I can not see how that is, as it is in a good part of New York, and that city is certainly not getting smaller."

"How do you account for the rents being less, then?"

"That is just the point. I can't account for it, and, to tell you the truth, I am suspicious of this real estate man."

"Who is he?"

"His name is Caleb Annister."

"What do you propose doing, dad? Can't you get a lawyer to see him, and find out if he is cheating you?"

"I suppose I could, but I have thought of a different plan. It came to me when I was lying sick here, and I decided to put it into operation, so as to straighten out my affairs as well as your own."

"What's your plan, dad?"

"I am going to send you to New York, to look up this property and the matter of rents, and see whether or not Caleb Annister is telling the truth, when he says that the value has gone down. Roy, I want you to act as my agent, and start for New York at once!"

CHAPTER III

A FAREWELL RIDE

His father's announcement rather startled Roy. He had never thought much of business, outside of that connected with the ranch, and now the idea of endeavoring to ascertain the value of property, and whether the agent of it was doing his duty, came as a sort of shock. But, more than this, was the idea of going to a big city.

In all his life, as far as he could remember, Roy had never been in any town of more than five thousand inhabitants. He had never, so far as he knew, taken more than a short ride in a railroad train. I say as far as he knew, for he had been born in Chicago, but when he was an infant, his parents had gone out west, so while it was true that he had lived in a big city, and had made quite a railroad journey, he knew nothing about it, except what his father had told him.

"You want me to go to New York, dad?" he repeated, wondering if he had heard aright.

"That's it. I want you to find out just exactly what Caleb Annister is doing."

"But, I have had no experience in those lines."

Frank V. Webster

"I know you have not, but I think you can do what I want. All it needs is brains and common sense, and you have both."

"But I have never been in a big city."

"No, not since you were old enough to notice anything, but that need not worry you. If I told you to go back to where the boys were rounding-up the cattle, you could do it; couldn't you?"

"Sure."

"Well, if you can find your way over the trackless plains I guess you can manage to get along in a big city, even if it is New York. All you have to do is to ask when you don't understand. I guess if some of those city boys came out here, they'd get lost a good deal quicker than you will in the streets of New York. Now you had better get ready to start. I'll draw up some papers, and get some instructions ready for you. I think Annister is trying to swindle you and me out of this property. If I was well enough I would go myself, but, as it is, I shall send you."

"Do you think you are well enough for me to leave you?" asked Roy anxiously.

"Oh, yes, there is nothing serious the matter with me. I shall have to be careful of what I eat, that's all, and if I went to New York I'd probably be worse off than I am here, for I would want to try all sorts of new dishes, and my dyspepsia would be very bad."

"Very well, dad. I'll get ready at once. It sure will be a new experience for me. I'll round-up this Caleb Annister for you, rope him and put the branding iron on, if I find he's trying to get any of our mavericks into his herd."

"That's the way to talk!" exclaimed Mr. Bradner. "You're a regular westerner, Roy. Don't let the ways of city folks bother you. Do the best you know how, be polite to the ladies, respectful to the men, and don't let 'em bluff you! Stick up for your rights, and don't be afraid of anybody. They may try to stampede you in New York, but you keep your head, and you'll come out all right."

"I'll try, dad. When do you want me to start?"

"To-morrow, if you can. The boys will be in from the round-up then."

That day Roy spent in getting his clothes packed in a big valise and a trunk. It was decided he should ride to the nearest railroad station, and there take a train for Chicago, where he would have to change cars for New York.

In the meanwhile Mr. Bradner drew up a paper giving his son the right to act in a certain capacity. This was put into legal form, and witnessed, a near-by notary being called in to attach his seal.

"Of course I don't know exactly how you will find the lay of the land there in New York," said Mr. Bradner that night, "as I have never been there. Nor do I know this Caleb Annister. I have had considerable correspondence with him, and I take him to be a sharp business man. He may try to bluff you, but don't you stand for it. It might be a good plan to size him up first, before you tell him who you are."

"That's what I'll do, dad."

"You'll have to make your own plans when you get there," went on his father. "You may have to spend considerable money, so I'll give you a good sum in cash, and a draft on my New York bankers. If you get in a hole do the best you can, and telegraph me if you need help. Just camp on the trail of this Caleb Annister, and see what his game is. It doesn't stand to reason that property in New York is shrinking in value. I think there is something wrong somewhere, and I depend on you to find it."

"I hope I won't disappoint you, dad."

"I don't believe you will, Roy. Now you had better get to bed, for it's quite late, and you'll have a hard journey ahead of you."

Roy did not feel a bit tired, for he was hardy and strong, but he did as his father suggested. He could not get to sleep at first thinking of his prospective trip, for he had always wanted to go to a big city, and now he had the chance.

Billy Carew and the other cowboys came in the next morning with the steers, which were turned into a corral for branding purposes. Roy told his friends of his journey.

"Prancing prairie dogs!" exclaimed Billy. "I wish I was going. Lickity thunder, but that's a great trip, clear to New York!"

"We'll ride to the station with you," proposed Bruce Arkdell. "We'll give you a good send off!"

"That's what we will!" chorused the others.

Roy was to start soon after dinner, as the Chicago express would not stop at the railroad station of Painted Stone unless it was flagged.

A little later a strange procession left the ranch house. Roy and Billy Carew rode at the head, and all the cowboys who could be spared followed after. Roy's trunk and valises were strapped on the back of a pack mule.

Mr. Bradner, who was not quite well enough to stand the trip to the station, bade his son an affectionate good-bye, and wished him all success.

"Telegraph if you get into trouble," he said.

"Yes, and we'll all hot-foot it to the burg of New York, and shoot-up the town!" exclaimed Billy. "We'll show 'em how a boy from the ranch can be took care of!"

"I guess there'll be no need of that," remarked Roy with a smile.

It was several miles to the railroad station, and, on the way the cowboys rushed their ponies here and there, indulging in all sorts of antics, for they regarded it as a sort of a holiday, though they liked Roy, and were sorry to see him leave.

"Now boys! Give him a grand salute!" proposed Bruce, when they came in sight of the station.

The cowboys drew their revolvers, aimed them into the air, and fired them off as fast as they could pull their triggers. It sounded as though a small battle was in progress.

"Give him a yell!" suggested Smoke Tardell, and the ranchers shouted like wild Indians.

"Here comes the train!" called Billy Carew, as a whistle was heard, and, down the long line of glistening rails, the smoke of a locomotive was seen. The station agent went out to flag the express.

"Take care of yourself," advised Bruce.

"Bring me back a slice of New York," requested Smoke. "I want it well done."

"Be careful you don't get 'well-done', Roy," advised Billy Carew. "Don't buy any gold bricks, or Confederate money, and take care, Roy, that them sharpers don't git ye!"

He waved his big sombrero, an example followed by all the other cowboys, as Roy climbed aboard the express. His trunk and valises were tumbled into the baggage car, the engineer blew two short blasts, and the train was off again, bearing Roy to New York.

His last view was of his father's cowboys, waving a farewell to him with their big hats, while some fired their revolvers, and others yelled at the top of their lungs.

"I wonder when I'll see them again," thought Roy. "I sort of hate to leave the old ranch, but I'm glad I'm going to New York."

He did not know all that was before him, nor what was to happen before he again saw his friends, the cowboys.

CHAPTER IV

ROY IS PUZZLED

While Roy's father had given him some instructions as to the best method of proceeding while in New York, Mr. Bradner had said nothing to his son about what he might expect on his railroad trip. Therefore the boy was totally unprepared for the novelties of modern travel. Mr. Bradner had thought it wise to let his son find out things for himself.

Roy had never been in anything but an ordinary day coach, and those were of an old-fashioned type. But his father had purchased for him tickets all the way to New York in the Pullman parlor and sleeping cars, and it was in a luxurious parlor car, then, that Roy found himself when he boarded the express.

At first the boy did not know what to make of it. The car had big chairs instead of the ordinary seats, the windows were nearly twice as large as those in other coaches, and there were silk and plush curtains hanging over them. Besides there was a thick, soft velvety carpet on the floor of the coach, and, what with the inlaid and polished wood, the hangings, mirrors, brass and nickel-plated fixtures, Roy thought he had, by mistake, gotten into the private car of some millionaire.

He had occasionally seen the outside of these fine coaches as they rushed through Painted Stone, but he had never dreamed that he would be in one. So, as soon as he entered the coach, he started back.

"What's de matter, sah?" inquired a colored porter in polite tones, as he came from what seemed a little cubby-hole built in the side of the car.

"Guess I'm in the wrong corral," remarked Roy, who was so used to using western and cattle terms, that he did not consider how they would sound to other persons.

"Wrong corral, sah?"

"Yes; I must be mixed in with the wrong brand. Where's the regular coach?"

"Oh, dis coach am all reg'lar, sah. Reg'lar as can be. We ain't got none but reg'lar coaches on dis yeah express. No indeed, sah."

"But I guess my ticket doesn't entitle me to a ride in a private car."

"Let me see youh ticket, sah."

Roy passed the negro the bit of pasteboard.

"Oh, yes indeedy, sah. Youh is all right. Dis am de coach youh g'wine to ride in. We goes all de way to Chicago, sah."

"Is this for regular passengers?" asked Roy, wondering how the railroad could afford to supply such luxurious cars.

"Well, it's fo' them as pays fo' it, sah. Youh has got a ticket fo' de Pullman car, an' dis am it, sah. Let me show yo' to youh seat, sah."

"Well, I s'pose it's all right," remarked Roy a little doubt-fully. He saw several passengers smiling, and he wondered if they were laughing at him, or if he had made a mistake. He resolved to be careful, as he did not want it known that he was making a long journey for the first time.

"Heah's youh seat," went on the porter, escorting Roy to a deep, soft chair. "I'll be right back yeah, an' if youh wants me, all youh has to do is push this yeah button," and he showed Roy an electric button fixed near the window.

"Well, I don't know what I'll want of you," said the boy, trying to think what excuse he could have for calling the colored man.

"Why, sah, youh might want to git breshed off, or youh might want a book, or a cigar—"

"I don't smoke," retorted Roy promptly.

"Well, I'm here to wait on passengers," went on the negro, "and if youh wants me all youh has to do is push that yeah button."

"All right—er—" he paused, not knowing what to call the porter.

"Mah name's George Washington Thomas Jefferson St. Louis Algernon Theophilus Brown, but folks dey gen'ally calls me George, sah," and the porter grinned so that he showed every one of his big white teeth.

"All right—George," said Roy, beginning to understand

something of matters. "I'll call you if I want you."

"Dey calls out when it's meal time."

"What's that?"

"I say dey calls out when it's meal time. De dining car potah will call out when it's time fo' dinner."

"Oh," remarked Roy, rather dubiously, for he did not know exactly what was meant.

The porter left him, laughing to himself at the lack of knowledge shown by the boy from the ranch, but for all that George Washington St. Louis Algernon Theophilus Brown resolved to do all he could for Roy. As for the young traveler he was so interested in the scenery, as it appeared to fly past the broad windows of the car, that he did not worry about what he was going to do when it came meal time.

Still, after an hour or so of looking out of the window it became a little tiresome, and he turned around to observe his fellow passengers. Seated near him was a well-dressed man, who had quite a large watch chain strung across his vest. He had a sparkling stone in his necktie, and another in a ring on his finger.

"Your first trip East?" he asked, nodding in a friendly way to Roy.

"My first trip, of any account, anywhere. I haven't taken a long railroad journey since I was a baby, and I don't remember that."

"I thought you looked as if you hadn't been a very great distance away from home. Going far?"

"To New York."

"Ah you have business there, I suppose?"

Now Roy, though he was but a youth, unused to the ways of the world, had much natural shrewdness. He had been brought up in the breeziness of the West, where it is not considered good form, to say the least, to ask too many questions of a man. If a person wanted to tell you his affairs, that was a different matter. So, as Roy's mission was more or less of a secret one, he decided it would not be well to talk about it, especially to strangers. So he answered:

"Yes, I have some business there."

His manner was such that the man soon saw the boy did not care to talk about his affairs, and, being a keen observer, too much so for Roy's good, as we shall soon see, the man did not pursue his questioning on those lines.

"Fine scenery," he remarked. "Good, open country around here."

Roy felt that was a safe enough subject to talk about, and he and the man, who introduced himself as Mr. Phelan Baker, spent some time in conversation.

Roy, however, was continually wondering what he should do when the announcement was made that dinner was to be served. He did not want to make any mistakes, and have the car full of passengers laugh at him, yet he did not know what was proper to do under the circumstances.

He had neglected to Inquire how they served meals on trains, and, in fact, had he done so, no one at the ranch could have told him, as not even Mr. Bradner had traveled enough to make it necessary to eat in a dining car.

"If I was back at the ranch I'd know what to do when I heard the grub-call," thought Roy. "But this thing has got me puzzled. It sure has. I wonder if they bring you in sandwiches and coffee, as they did to a party I went to? Or do you have to go up and help yourself? I don't see how they cook anything on a train going as fast as this one. They must have to eat cold victuals. Well, I guess I can stand it for a few days, I've eaten cold bacon and bread when on a roundup, and I'm not going to hold back now. Guess I'll just do as the rest do."

A little while after this a colored man, in a spotless white suit, passed through the parlor car, calling out:

"Dinner is now being served in the dining car. First call for dinner!"

"Well, it's up to me to go to grub now," thought Roy. "I wonder how I'll make out?"

CHAPTER V

A QUEER BED

"Are you going to eat on the first call?" asked Mr. Baker, rising from his comfortable chair and looking at Roy.

"I don't know—I think—Yes, I guess I will."

It suddenly occurred to the boy that he might take advantage of the acquaintance he had formed with the man, and observe just how he ought to conduct himself in the dining car.

"I shall be glad of your company," spoke Mr. Baker, with a pleasant smile. "Will you sit at my table?"

"I'm not so very hungry," remarked Roy, thinking that if he found things too strange he could call for something simple, though the truth was he had an excellent appetite.

"I am not either," declared Mr. Baker. "I never eat much while traveling, but I think it best to have my meals regularly. Now, if you'll come with me, we'll see what they have at this traveling hotel."

He led the way from the parlor to the dining car. If Roy had been astonished at the magnificence of the first coach he was doubly so at the scene which now met his eyes.

Arranged along both sides of the dining car, next to the broad, high windows, were small tables, sparkling with cut-glass and silver. In the center of each table was a small pot of graceful ferns, while throughout the car there were fine hangings, beautifully inlaid wood, and on the floor a soft carpet. It was, indeed, a fine traveling hotel.

At the tables, not all of which were occupied, were seated beautiful women, some handsomely gowned, and there were men, attired in the height of fashion. For the first time Roy felt rather ashamed of his ordinary "store" clothes, which were neither properly cut, nor of good material.

"Here is a good table," said Mr. Baker, indicating one about the center of the car.

Roy took his seat opposite his new acquaintance, a queer feeling of nervousness overcoming him.

"I'd rather ride a bucking bronco any day, than be here," the boy thought. But he was not going to back out now. He knew he had the money to pay for whatever he ordered, and, he reflected that if he was not as stylishly dressed as the others, he was probably more hungry than any of them, for he had an early breakfast.

As soon as Roy and Mr. Baker were seated, a colored waiter glided swiftly to their table and filled their glasses from a curiously shaped vessel, called a "caraffe," which looked something like a bottle or flask, with a very large body, and a very small neck. Inside was a solid lump of ice, which made the water cold. Roy looked curiously at the piece of frozen crystal. Mr. Baker noted his look of astonishment.

"Don't you like ice water?" he asked.

"Yes, but I was wondering how in the world they ever got that big hunk of ice through the little neck of that bottle."

"Oh," exclaimed Mr. Baker with a laugh, "they first fill the caraffe with water, and then they freeze it in an ice machine they have on the train for keeping the other supplies from spoiling. It would be rather difficult to put that chunk of ice down through that narrow neck."

Roy understood now. He began to think he had lots to learn of the world, but there was more coming. The waiter placed a menu card in front of Mr. Baker, and laid one at Roy's plate. He knew what they were, for he had several times taken dinner at a small hotel at Painted Stone.

He was not prepared however for the queer language in which the menu card or bill of fare was printed. It was French, and the names of the most ordinary dishes were in that foreign tongue.

Roy was puzzled. He wanted a substantial meal, but he did not know how to order it. He was afraid to try to pronounce the odd looking words, and I am afraid if he had done so he would have made a mistake, as, indeed, better educated persons than he would have done. He had a wild notion of telling the waiter to bring everything on the bill of fare, but there seemed to be too many dishes.

Finally he decided on a course to pursue. The waiter was standing there, polite and all attention, for, though Roy's clothes did not impress him as indicating a lad of wealth, Mr. Baker's attire was showy enough to allow the colored man to think he might receive a handsome tip.

"I think I'll have a ham sandwich and a cup of coffee," said Roy in desperation. He knew he was safe in ordering that, even if it was not on the card, though it might have been for all he knew, disguised under some odd name.

Mr. Baker looked surprised.

"I should say you hadn't any appetite," he remarked. Then, as he understood the situation, and Roy's embarrassment, he said: "Suppose I order for both of us? I am used to this sort of thing."

Roy was grateful for this delicate way of putting it, and, with a sigh of relief, he replied:

"I wish you would. I guess I've got a good appetite after all."

Thereupon Mr. Baker ordered a simple but substantial meal, including soup, fish, roast beef, potatoes and side dishes of vegetables, ending up with coffee and pie.

"This is fine!" exclaimed Roy, when he had finished. "I s'pose they charge about two dollars for grub like this?"

Several persons in the dining car smiled, for Roy was used to shouting at cattle, and calling to cowboys, and had acquired a habit of speaking in rather loud tones.

"No, this 'grub' will cost you one dollar," said Mr. Baker.

"Well, it's worth it," declared the boy, pulling out quite a roll of bills, for his father had been generous. At the sight of the money a greedy look came into the eyes of Mr. Baker, a look that would have warned Roy had he seen it. But he was busy looking for a one-dollar bill among the fives and tens.

"Now, if you're ready we'll go back to the parlor car, and have a cigar in the smoking room," suggested Mr. Baker.

"No, thank you. Not for mine. I don't smoke."

"Well, it is a useless habit I suppose, but I am too old to change now. I'll join you presently," and the man went into a small compartment at one end of the parlor car, when they reached it, leaving Roy to go to his chair alone.

Had the boy seen the three men whom Mr. Baker greeted in the smoking room, perhaps our hero would not have been quite so ready to continue his acquaintance with the man. For, in the little apartment were three individuals whose faces did not indicate any too much honesty, and whose clothes were on the same "flashy" order as were Mr. Baker's, though none of the trio had as expensive jewelry as had Roy's new friend.

"Well, sport, how about you?" asked one of the men. "Did you manage to pick up anything?"

"Not so loud, Ike," cautioned Mr. Baker, addressing the man who had spoken, and whose name was Isaac Sutton. "I think I can put you on the track of something."

"Something good?" asked the third man, who was known as Jerome Hynard, though that was not his real name.

"We want it with plenty of cash," added the last man, who was called Dennison Tupper.

"This is a green kid, right from the ranch, going to New York," said Phelan Baker. "He's got quite a wad of money, and if you work the game right you may be able to get the most of it. I'll tell you how."

Then the four began to whisper, for they were laying a plot and were afraid of being overheard. All unconscious of the danger that threatened him, Roy was back in the parlor car, enjoying the scenery, and thinking of the many strange things he would see in New York.

For some reason Mr. Baker did not come back where Roy was. Perhaps he feared the boy might be suspicious of his sudden friendship, for Mr. Baker was a good reader of character, and he saw that Roy, in spite of his lack of experience, was a shrewd lad.

As for the young traveler, he began to get tired. He was unused to sitting still so long, and riding in a soft chair was very different from being on the back of the swift pony, galloping over the plains.

"I wonder what they're going to do about bunks?" thought Roy, as he looked about the car. "I don't fancy sleeping on these chairs, and I've heard they made the seats in the coaches up into bunks."

Roy had never seen a sleeping car, and imagined the coach he was in was one. He decided he would ask the porter about it soon, if he saw no signs of the beds being made up. He had his supper alone at a table in the dining car, Mr. Baker remaining with his three cronies, and out of Roy's sight. Profiting by his experience at dinner, the boy knew how to order a good meal.

To his relief, soon after he got back to the parlor car, the porter who had first spoken to him, came up and announced:

"Youh berth will be ready any time youh want it, sah."

"Berth?"

"Yais, sah."

Roy did not know exactly what was meant. At the ranch that word was never used, a bed being a "bunk."

"I don't think I care for any," said Roy, deciding that was the safest way.

"What's that, sah? Youh ain't goin to sit up all night, be youh? Mighty uncomfortable, sah. Better take a bed. Youh ticket calls fo' one, sah."

"Oh, you mean a bunk?"

"Bunk! Ha! Ha! Youh western gen'men gwine to hab youh joke, I see. We calls 'em berths, sah."

"Is mine ready?"

"Jest as soon as youh want it. Youh can go back in de sleeping car."

This Roy understood. He went back two coaches toward the rear, as directed by the porter, and found himself in still another kind of car. This had big plush seats, like small couches, facing each other, while, overhead, was a sort of sloping ceiling.

"I don't see where there are many bunks here," the boy remarked to himself. He saw persons sitting in the seats, talking, and, finding one unoccupied, he took possession of it. Soon a porter came in to him, examined his ticket, and asked:

"Do youh wish youh berth made up now, sah?"

"Guess I might as well," replied Roy, wondering where the porter was going to get the bed from, and whether he was going to produce it from some unseen source, as a conjurer pulls rabbits out of tall hats.

"Ef youh jest kindly take the next seat, I'll make up your berth," said the porter, and Roy moved back one place, but where he could still watch the colored man.

That individual then proceeded to make up the berth. While the process is familiar to many of my young readers, it was a novelty to Roy. With much wonder he watched the man lift up the cushions of the seats, take out blankets and pillows from the hollow places, and then slide the two bottoms of the seats together until they made a level place.

Then what Roy had thought to be merely a slanting part of the ceiling was pulled down, revealing a broad shelf, that formed the upper berth or bed. On this shelf were sheets, blankets and other things needed for the beds. In a short time Roy saw made before his eyes, where there had been only seats before, a comfortable "bunk" with pillows, white sheets, blankets, curtains hanging down in front and all complete.

"Now youh can turn in," said the porter with a smile, as he began to make up another berth. Roy decided to wait a while, until he saw how other men travelers undressed, and when he saw one man retire behind the curtains, and, sitting on the edge of his berth, take off his shoes, and the heavier parts of his clothing, Roy did likewise. Thus the difficult problem of getting to bed was solved.

CHAPTER VI

A SUDDEN AWAKENING

Stretching out in the comfortable berth Roy thought he would soon fall asleep, as he was quite tired. But the novelty of his ride, the strange sensation of being whirled along many miles an hour while lying in bed, proved too much for him, and he found himself still wide-awake, though he had been in the berth an hour or more.

The noise of the wheels, the rumble of the train, the click-clack as the wheels passed over rail joints or switches, the bumping and swaying motion, all served to drive sleep away from Roy's eyes.

He thought of many things, of what he would do when he got to New York, of his father, of Caleb Annister, and what he should say to the New Yorker. Finally, however, the very monotony of the noises began to make him feel drowsy. In a little while he found his eyes closing, and then, almost before he knew it, he was asleep.

Meanwhile, back in the smoking room, the three men and Mr. Baker were talking over their cigars. One of them produced a pack of cards, and they began to play.

"Maybe if Isaac's game doesn't work, we can get him with these," suggested Mr. Baker, as he dealt the pasteboards to his companions.

"Maybe," agreed Hynard. "What time is Ike going to try it?"

"About two o'clock. He'll be sure to be asleep then."

Back in his berth, some hours after this, Roy was dreaming that he was being shaken in his bunk at the ranch house. He thought Billy Carew was urging him to get up early to go off on a round-up, and Roy was trying to drive the sleep away from his eyes, and comply.

Suddenly he knew it was not a dream, but that some one was moving him, though very gently. Then he became aware that a hand was being cautiously thrust under his pillow.

Roy did not stop to think—he acted. His instant impression was of thieves, and he did the most natural thing under the circumstances. He grabbed the hand that was being gently shoved under his pillow.

Instantly the wrist, which his fingers clasped, was snatched away, withdrawn from the curtains, and a voice exclaimed:

"Beg pardon. I was looking for your ticket. I'm the conductor. It's all right."

Roy thought the voice did not sound a bit like the voice of the conductor, who had spoken to him some time before. Nor could the boy understand why a conductor should be feeling under his pillow for his ticket, when Roy had, as was the custom, given him the bits of pasteboard, including his berth check, earlier in the evening. The conductor had said he would keep them until morning, to avoid the necessity of waking Roy up to look at them during the night.

"That's queer," thought the boy.

He sat up in bed, and thrust his head through the curtains that hung down in front of his berth. Down the aisle, which was dimly lighted, he saw a man hurrying toward the end of the car—the end where the smoking apartment was.

"That wasn't the conductor," said Roy to himself. "He has two brass buttons on the back of coat, and this chap hasn't any. I believe he was a thief, after my money. Lucky I didn't put it under my pillow, or he'd have it now. I must be on the watch. No wonder Billy Carew warned me to be careful. I wonder who that fellow was?"

Roy had half a notion to get up and inform a porter or the conductor what had happened, but he did not like to dress in the middle of the night, and go hunting through the sleeping car for someone to speak to about the matter.

"I'll just be on the watch," thought Roy, "and if he comes back I'll be ready for him."

However, he was not further disturbed that night, and soon fell asleep again, not forgetting, however, the precaution of hiding his pocketbook in the middle of his bed, under the blankets, where, if thieves tried to take it, they would first have to get him out of the berth.

Roy awakened shortly after sunrise the next morning. He was accustomed to early rising at the ranch, and this habit still clung to him. He managed to dress, while sitting on the edge of his berth, and then he reached down under the edge of it on the floor of the car, where, the night before, he had left his shoes. To his surprise they were gone.

Frank V. Webster

"That's funny," he thought. "I wonder if the fellow who didn't get my money, took my shoes for spite?"

To make sure he stepped out into the aisle in his stocking feet, and looked under his berth. His shoes were not to be seen.

"Now I am in a pickle," thought the boy. "How am I going all the way to New York without shoes? I can't go out in my stocking feet to get a new pair, and I don't suppose there are any stores near the stations, where I could buy new ones. But that's the only thing I can do. I wonder if the train would wait long enough until I could send one of the porters to a store for a pair of shoes? It would be a funny thing to do, I guess, and, besides, he wouldn't know what size to get. I certainly am up against it!"

As Roy stood in the curtained aisle of the car, all alone, for none of the other travelers were up yet, he saw a colored porter approaching. Something in the boy's manner prompted the man to ask:

"Can I do anything fo' youh, sah? You'se up early, sah."

"I am looking for my shoes."

"Oh, youh shoes. I took 'em, sah."

"You took 'em? What right have you taking my shoes? Haven't you got any of your own?" and Roy spoke sternly, for he thought this was too much; first an attempt made to rob him of his money, and then some one stealing his shoes.

"Where are they?" he went on. "I want 'em."

"Yais, sah. Right away, sah. I jest took 'em a little while ago to blacken 'em, sah. I allers does that to the gen'men's shoes. I'll have 'em right back. Did youh think I done stole 'em, sah?"

"That's what I did," replied Roy with a smile. "I thought I'd have to go to New York in my stocking feet."

"Ob, no indeedy, sah. I allers goes around and collects the gen'men's shoes early, 'fore they gits up. I takes 'em back to my place and I blacks 'em. Den I brings 'em back."

"That's quite an idea," said Roy, now noticing that from under the berths of his fellow travelers the shoes were all missing.

"Yais, sah," went on the colored man. "And sometimes, sah, sometimes, youh know, de gen'men's gives me a little remembrance, sah, for blackenin' their shoes."

"Then I'll do the same," spoke Roy, remembering what Billy Carew had told him of the necessity for "tipping" the car porters.

"Thank youh, sah. I'll have youh shoes back d'rectly, sah."

The porter was as good as his word, and soon Roy was able to put on his shoes, which he hardly recognized. The dust that had accumulated from his ride across the plains to the railroad depot had all been removed, and the leather shone brightly. He gave the porter a quarter of a dollar, for which the colored man returned profuse thanks. Soon the other travelers began to get up. Roy watched them go to the washroom and did likewise. He met Mr. Baker in there, and accepted an invitation to go to breakfast with him in the dining car.

"Did you sleep well last night?" asked the man with the big watch chain.

"Pretty well," replied Roy, deciding to say nothing of the hand that was thrust under his pillow. He first wanted to make a few observations of his fellow passengers.

After breakfast, when Roy was sitting in his chair in the parlor car, Mr. Baker approached.

"There are some friends of mine in the smoking room," he said to the boy. "I would like to introduce you to them."

"That is very kind of you," replied the young traveler. "I shall be glad to meet them," for Roy considered it nice on the part of Mr. Baker to take so much interest in him.

"We can have a pleasant chat together," went on the man as he led the way to a private room or "section" as they are called. This was near the smoking room end of the car. "My friends are much interested in ranch life, and perhaps you will give them some information."

CHAPTER VII

A GAME ON THE TRAIN

The three men in the compartment looked up as Phelan Baker and Roy entered. They exchanged significant glances, but the boy from the ranch did not notice them. Then the men made room for the new-comers on the richly upholstered couches.

"Ah, how are you, Baker?" said Isaac Sutton. "Glad to see you."

"Allow me to introduce a friend of mine," said Mr. Baker presenting Roy to the three men in turn. "He can tell you all you want to know about ranch life," for, by skillful questioning Mr. Baker had learned more about Roy than the lad was aware he had told.

"That's good," remarked Jerome Hynard. "I may decide to buy a ranch, some day."

"Would you say it was a healthy sort of life?" asked Dennison Tupper, who was quite pale, and looked as if he had some illness.

"It was very healthy out where I was," answered Roy.

"I guess one look at you proves that," put in Mr. Baker, in an admiring tone. "You seem as strong and hardy as a young ox."

"Yes, and I eat like one, when I'm on a round-up," said the boy.

There was considerable more conversation, the men asking Roy many questions about western life, and showing an interest in the affairs of the ranch. Roy answered them to the best of his ability, and naturally was pleased that the men should think him capable of giving them information.

Finally, when the conversation began to lag a bit, Dennison Tupper remarked:

"Perhaps our young friend would have no objections if we gentlemen played a game of cards to pass away the time."

"Certainly I have no objections to your playing," said Roy, who had often watched the cowboys at the ranch play various games.

Once more the four men exchanged glances. Mr. Baker produced a pack of cards and soon the travelers were deep in the game. They did not seem to be gambling, only playing for "fun" as they called it.

"Oh, I believe I'm tired. I'm going to drop out," suddenly remarked Mr. Baker.

"Oh, don't do that," expostulated Sutton.

"No, you'll break up the game," remonstrated Tupper.

"Of course. Three can't play whist very well," added Hynard

in rather ungracious tones. "Be a good fellow and stay in the game, Baker."

"No, I'm tired."

"Perhaps our young friend from the ranch will take your place," suggested Sutton. "Will you—er—Mr. Bradner? We'll play for love or money, just as you like. You must be a sport—all the western chaps are. Come on, sit in the game, take Mr. Baker's place and don't let it break up."

It was a cunning appeal, addressed both to Roy's desire to be of service to his new friends, and also to his vanity. Fortunately he was proof against both. Roy had watched the men playing cards, and, to his mind they showed altogether too much skill. They acted more like regular gamblers than like persons playing to pass away an idle hour. He was at once suspicious.

"No, thank you," he said. "I never play cards, for love or money."

Something seemed to annoy at least three of the men, and they looked at Mr. Baker.

"Why I thought you said—" began Tupper, winking at the man who had first made Roy's acquaintance.

"Dry up!" exclaimed Hynard. "That's all right," he added quickly to the boy. "We don't want any one to play against his will. It's all right. We only thought maybe you'd like to pass away the time. I dare say Baker will stick in the game now."

"Oh, yes, I'll stay to oblige you, but I don't care for it," and pretending to suppress a yawn, Mr. Baker again took his seat at the small card table. A little later Roy left the apartment, going back to his place in the parlor car.

"I don't like those three men," he said to himself. "I believe they are professional gamblers. Mr. Baker seems nice, but I wouldn't trust the others."

As for the four men whom Roy had left, they seemed to lose all interest in their game, after the boy from the ranch was out of sight.

"Humph!" exclaimed Hynard. "That didn't work, did it?"

"No more than Isaac's attempt last night to get—" began Tupper, but Sutton silenced him with a gesture.

"Hush! Not so loud!" he said. "Some one may hear you."

"Leave it to me," said Mr. Baker. "I think I can get him into something else soon. You fellows lay low until I give you the tip."

The rest of that morning Roy saw nothing of the men whose acquaintance he had made. He got into conversation with several other passengers, some of whom were interesting characters. One man, who had traveled extensively, pointed out, along the way, the various scenes of note, telling Roy something about them.

It was after dinner when Mr. Phelan Baker, followed by his three friends, entered the parlor car. They took seats near where Roy had chanced to rest.

"Traveling is rather dull, isn't it?' began Mr. Baker.

"I don't find it so," replied Roy.

"No, that's because it's your first journey. Wait until you have crossed the continent a dozen times, and you'll begin to wish you'd never seen it."

"It seems to me there is always something of interest," said the boy.

"Probably there is, if your eyesight is good, and you can see it. I'm getting along in years, and I can't see objects as well as I once could."

"I suppose you must have pretty good eyesight, haven't you?" asked Sutton, abruptly taking part in the conversation. Roy and the four men were all alone in one end of the car, the other passengers, with but few exceptions, having gotten off at various stations.

"Well, I reckon I don't need glasses to see the brand on a steer," replied Roy.

"That's so, and I guess you have to be pretty quick to distinguish the different branding marks, don't you?"

"You do when you're cutting out a bunch of cattle after a round-up. They keep moving around so it's hard to tell which are yours, and which belong to another ranch."

"What did I tell you?" asked Sutton in triumph of Hynard, who sat next to him.

"Well, you're right," admitted the other.

Roy looked a little surprised at this conversation. Mr. Baker explained.

"My two friends here were having a little dispute about

eyesight," he said. "Mr. Sutton said you had the best eyesight of any one he ever saw, and were quick to notice anything. He said you had to be to work on a cattle range."

"And Mr. Hynard said he believed he had as good eyesight as you," put in Tupper.

"I told him he hadn't, and we agreed to ask you," went on Sutton.

"That's all right. His saying so doesn't prove it," remarked Hynard, in a somewhat surly tone.

"Of course not, but it doesn't take much to see that he has better eyesight than you, and is quicker with it. He has to be to use a lasso, don't you, Mr. Bradner?"

"Well, it does take a pretty quick eye and hand to get a steer when he's on the run," admitted Roy.

"And you can do it, I'll bet. Hynard, you're not in it with this lad."

"I believe I am!"

"Now don't get excited," advised Mr. Baker, in soothing tones. "We can easily settle this matter."

"How? We haven't got a lasso here, nor a wild steer," said Hynard. "Anyhow I don't claim I can throw a lariat as well as he can. I only said I had as quick eyesight."

"Well, we can prove that," went on Mr. Baker.

"How?"

"Easy money. Let's see. This windowsill will do."

From his pocket Mr. Baker produced three halves of English walnut shells, and a small black ball, about the size of a buck shot. It seemed to be made of rubber.

"Here's a little trick that will prove any one's eyesight," he said. "The eye doctors in New York use it to test any person who needs glasses. A doctor friend of mine gave me this."

"How do you work it?" asked Hynard, seemingly much interested.

"This way. I place these three shells on the windowsill, so. Then I put the little ball under one. Watch me closely. I move it quite fast, first putting it under one shell, then the other. Now, I stop and, Hynard, tell me which shell it's under! I don't believe you can, I think my young friend can do so."

"All right," agreed Hynard.

"Which shell is the ball under?" asked Mr. Baker, drawing back, and leaving the three shells in a row; they all looked alike, yet Roy was sure the ball was under the middle one.

"It's under there!" exclaimed Hynard, putting his finger on the end shell nearest Roy.

"Is it?" asked Mr. Baker with a laugh, as he raised it up, and showed nothing beneath. "Now let Mr. Bradner try."

"I think it's there," spoke the boy, indicating the middle shell.

"Right you are," came from Mr. Baker, as he lifted the shell, and disclosed the ball.

"Well, it's easier to pick the right one out of two, than out of three," remonstrated Hynard.

"All right. I'll give him first pick this time," and once more Mr. Baker manipulated the shells and ball.

"Now where is it?" he asked Roy quickly. The boy, who was quite taken with the new trick, was eagerly leaning forward, watching with eyes that little escaped, the movements of Mr. Baker's fingers.

"It's there," he said quietly, indicating the shell farthest away from him.

"What did I tell you?" asked Mr. Baker, lifting the shell and showing that Roy was right.

"He's got you beat, Hynard," said Sutton.

"Well, I'll bet he can't do it again."

Roy did, much to his own amusement.

"I'll tell you what I'll do," said Hynard suddenly. "I'll bet you five dollars I can do it this time, Baker."

"Very well, I'll go you."

The money was put up, the shells shifted, and Hynard made his choice. He got the right shell.

"There's where I lose five dollars," said Mr. Baker, with regret, passing the bill to Hynard.

"You try him," whispered Tupper to Roy. "You can guess right every time. Bet him ten dollars. You can't make money easier."

All at once the real meaning of what had just taken place was revealed to Roy. The men wanted him to gamble, under the guise of a trick. And he was sharp enough to know that once he bet any money, the shell he would pick out would have no ball under it. In fact, had he taken the bait and bet, Mr. Baker, by a sleight-of-hand trick, would not have put the ball under any shell so that, no matter which one Roy selected, he would have been wrong, and would have lost, though they might have let him win once or twice, just to urge him on. Understanding what the trick was, he exclaimed:

"I don't think I care to bet any money. I have proved that I have quick eyesight, and I think that's all you wanted to know," and, turning away he went back to his chair, at the farther end of the car.

CHAPTER VIII

A STOP FOR REPAIRS

For a few seconds the four men were too surprised to say anything. They stood looking at each other and, when they had gone to the smoking room, with an angry glance at Mr. Baker, Sutton remarked:

"I thought you said the kid would bite at this game?"

"I thought he would."

"Well, you've got another 'think' coming."

"Yes, you've bungled this thing all the way through," added Hynard.

"I didn't blunder any more than you did. I'd like to know who first made his acquaintance, and found out he had money."

"Well, you did that part of it, but he's got his money yet, and we haven't," said Tupper.

"And we're not likely to get it," went on Hynard. "I think he'll be suspicious of us after this."

"Maybe not," remarked Sutton, hopefully. "We may be able to get him into some other kind of a game. If we can't—"

He did not finish, but the other men knew what he meant. Roy had incurred the enmity of some dangerous characters, and it behooved him to be on the lookout.

The boy had not been in his seat many minutes before an elderly gentleman, the one who had been describing the various scenes of interest, came up to him.

"Did I see you playing some game with those men just now?" he asked.

"They were showing me a game," answered Roy. "They said they wanted to test my quick eyesight."

"What was it?"

"It was a game with three shells and a small ball."

"I thought so. My boy, do you know what that game is called?"

"No, sir, but I didn't care to play it the way they wanted me to. They wanted me to bet money."

"And you refused?"

"I sure did."

"That is where you were right. That is an old swindling trick, called the 'shell game'. If you had bet any money you would have lost."

"I thought as much," said Roy. "I'm not so green as I look,

even if I spent all my life on a ranch."

"Indeed you are not, I am glad to see. I would advise you not to have anything more to do with those men."

"Do you know them?"

"No, but they have the ways and airs of professional gamblers."

"They tried to rope me up, I guess," said Roy. "But they didn't have rope enough to tie me. Now I know their brand I'll sure be careful not to mix in with 'em."

"I don't exactly understand your terms. I—"

"I beg your pardon," said Roy. "I suppose I talk, more or less, as I do on the ranch. I meant they tried to get me into one of their corrals and take my hide off. Hold me up, you know."

"I'm afraid I don't exactly know," went on the gentleman with a smile, "but I gather that you mean they would have robbed you, after getting you into their power."

"That's it," said Roy. "I'm on another trail now, and they want to be careful," and he looked as though he could take care of himself, a fact that the gentleman noticed.

"I felt like warning you, my boy," he said, "as I saw it was your first long journey."

"And I'm much obliged to you," said Roy. "I wonder how everyone knows I'm a tenderfoot when it comes to traveling on railroad trains?"

"A tenderfoot?"

"Yes, that's what we call persons who don't know much about western life. I suppose their feet get tender from taking such long walks on the plains. Anyhow that means a sort of 'greenhorn' I suppose. Everyone on the train spots me for that."

"Well, it is easy to see you are not used to traveling, for you take so much interest in everything, and you show that it is new to you. But you are learning fast. Even an experienced traveler might have been taken in by those gamblers."

"I guess they'll not bother me any more," said Roy.

And he was right, but only to a certain extent, for, though the gamblers did not "bother" him again, he had not seen the last of them, as you shall see.

The tricksters were in a bad mood, and, soon after that they left the smoking room, and remained in another car, so Roy did not see them again that day.

The express continued on, bringing the boy nearer and nearer to Chicago. He wished he might have a little time to spend there, as he had heard much of it, especially the stock yards, where his father sent many head of cattle in the course of a year. But Roy knew he must hurry on to New York, to attend to the business on which he had been sent.

The next morning, soon after breakfast, the train came to a sudden stop, near a small railroad station. As the express did not stop, except at the large cities, Roy wondered if some one like himself, had flagged the engineer. Soon he was aware, however, that something unusual had occurred. Passengers began leaving their seats, and went out of the cars.

"I wonder what's the matter?" Roy said aloud. He was overheard by the gentleman who had talked to him about the gamblers, and who had given his name, as John Armstrong.

"I think we've had an accident," said Mr. Armstrong.

"An accident? Is anybody killed?"

"No, I do not think so. Suppose we get out and see what the trouble is?"

They left their seats, and joined the other passengers who were walking toward the head of the train, which was a long one. It did not take many seconds to ascertain that an accident had occurred to the engine of the express, and that it would be necessary to send to the next station to get materials to make repairs.

"That means we'll be held here for some time," observed Mr. Armstrong. "Well, if the delay is not too long, it will give you a chance to walk about and stretch your muscles."

"And I'll be glad enough to do it," replied Roy. "I'm not used to sitting still, and it sure is very tiresome to me. I'd like to have my pony, Jack Rabbit, here now. I'd take a fine gallop."

"Well, I think a walk will have to answer in place of it now. There does not seem to be much in the way of amusements at this station."

The depot was a mere shanty, with a small telegraph and ticket office in it. A few houses and a store made up the "town," which was located on the plains.

As Roy started toward the depot many of the passengers got back in their cars, as the sun was hot. Roy, however, rather enjoyed it. Among those who had alighted were Mr. Baker and his three cronies. They stood on the depot platform, talking together.

"Maybe they're trying to get up some new scheme to get me to gamble," thought Roy. As he neared the station his attention was attracted by a rather curious figure.

This was a young man whom Roy at once characterized as a "dude," for he and the cowboys had been in the habit of so calling any one who was as well dressed as was the stranger. And Roy at once knew that the man had not been on the train before, as the boy from the ranch had seen all the passengers during his journey.

The "tenderfoot", as Roy also characterized him, was attired in a light suit, the trousers very much creased. He had on a purple necktie, rather a high collar, and patent leather shoes. In his hand he carried a light cane, and in one eye was a glass, called a monocle. Beside him was a dress-suit case, and he looked as if he was ready to travel.

Roy glanced at him, and was inclined to smile at the elaborate costume of the youth, for the western lad had the usual cattleman's contempt for fashionable clothes, arguing (not always rightly) that a person who paid so much attention to dress could not amount to a great deal.

The young man stood leaning against the side of the depot, carelessly swinging his cane. Roy could see he had a valuable watch chain across his vest, and, in his tie there sparkled what was presumably a diamond.

As Roy watched he saw Baker and his three cronies approach the "dude." A moment later they had engaged him in conversation.

Frank V. Webster

"I'll bet they're up to some game," mused Roy. "I wonder if I can find out what it is, and spoil it? I believe they will try to get the best of that 'tenderfoot.' Guess I'll see what's up."

CHAPTER IX

THE DUDE IS SWINDLED

Carelessly, so as not to attract the attention of the four men, Roy strolled to the depot platform, taking care to get on the side opposite that on which was the elaborately-dressed youth. The sharpers did not see Roy, who kept in the shadow, and the attention of the other passengers from the train was taken up with what the engineer and firemen were doing, to get the locomotive ready for the repair crew.

"How do you do?" asked Mr. Baker, of the "tenderfoot," as he approached with his three cronies. "Haven't I met you somewhere before?"

"Well, really, I couldn't say; don't you know," replied the well-dressed youth, with an affected drawl.

"I am sure I have," went on Mr. Baker. "So are my three friends. As soon as we saw you standing here, my friend, Mr. Sutton, said to me, 'Where have I seen that distinguished looking gentleman before?' Didn't you, Sutton?"

"Indeed I did, Mr. Baker. And Mr. Hynard said the same thing."

"Sure I did," replied Mr. Hynard. "I know I've met you before Mr.—er—Ah, I didn't quite catch the name."

"My name is De Royster—Mortimer De Royster, of New York," replied the dude, seemingly much flattered at the attention he had attracted. "I'm sure I can't recall where I met you gentlemen before, but, don't you know, your faces are very familiar to me."

"Of course," went on Mr. Baker. "I remember you very well now. You are a son of Van Dyke De Royster, the great New York banker; are you not?"

"No," replied Mr. De Royster, "he is only a distant relative of mine, but I belong to the same family. It is very distinguished."

"Indeed it is," said Mr. Baker. "I have often read in history of the great doings of the De Roysters. Gentlemen, shake hands with Mr. De Royster. I know his relative, the great banker, Van Dyke De Royster, very well."

Now this was true, to a certain extent, but all the acquaintance Mr. Baker had with the well known banker, was when the latter had him arrested for trying to cash a forged check. But Mr. Baker did not mention this.

"I am very glad to meet you," said Mortimer De Royster, as he shook hands with the four swindlers, thinking them delightful gentlemen indeed.

"Are you going far?" asked Hynard.

"To New York. You see I am—er—that is—er—I have been doing a little business—I am selling jewelry for a relative of mine in New York. It is not exactly work, for I am traveling for my health, and I do a little trade on the side."

"Guess he's ashamed to let it be known that he works for a living," thought Roy, but later he found he had misjudged De Royster.

"Ah, in the jewelry line, eh?" asked Mr. Baker. "I used to be in that myself."

He did not mention that the way he was "in it" was to try to swindle a diamond merchant out of some precious stones, in which he was partly successful.

"Did you do any business in this section?" asked Tupper.

"Not much. I stopped off to see some friends, and I did not try to sell them anything. I don't do business with my friends—I don't think it dignified, don't you know," and Mortimer De Royster swung his cane with a jaunty air, and tried to twirl the ends of a very short mustache.

"That's right; I can see you're the right stuff," remarked Mr. Baker, with a wink at his companions. "Did you come down here to take the train?"

"Yes, I am on my way to New York."

"How do you find trade?" asked Mr. Baker.

"Well, really, it is not very good, but that does not annoy me, as I am only doing this as a side line. I don't worry, don't you know."

"I see. You're a sport!" exclaimed Tupper, with easy familiarity. "I sized you up for a sport as soon as I saw you. I must have met you in New York."

"Yes, I make my headquarters there," said the salesman. "I seem to remember you. Sporting life is very attractive to me, I assure you, really it is."

"That's the way to talk!" put in Hynard. "Be a sport!"

"They're flattering him for some purpose," thought Roy. "I wonder what their object is."

He was hidden around the corner of the depot, where he could hear without being seen.

"That's a very fine watch chain you have on," said Mr. Baker. "It is much better than mine."

"And I guess he has a better watch than yours, too, Baker," spoke up Sutton, with a wink, which Mr. De Royster did not see.

"No, he hasn't. My watch cost five hundred dollars."

"I have a very fine timepiece, I don't mind admitting," spoke the well-dressed youth. "It was given to me by my father, who is quite wealthy."

"I'd like to see it," said Mr. Baker.

By this time an engine, with some parts to repair the broken locomotive, had arrived from a near-by freight yard. The train crew had made the adjustments, and the express was almost ready to proceed. Nearly all the passengers, who had alighted, had again boarded their cars.

"I shall be pleased to show you my watch," said Mr. De Royster, drawing out a heavy gold affair. "I think you will readily agree with me, that it is a valuable one."

He passed it to Mr. Baker, and, from where he stood Roy could see the swindler slip it into his pocket and substitute for it one somewhat like it, but, probably made of brass instead of gold. Mr. Baker turned his back, pretending to be trying to get a good light, while he compared his watch with that of Mr. De Royster.

"That's a fine diamond pin in your tie," said Tupper, indicating the stone in the salesman's tie.

"Yes. Would you like to look at it? It is of very pure color."

He drew out the gem, and, unsuspectingly passed it to Tupper.

At that instant the locomotive engineer blew two warning whistles, so that the lagging passengers might get on the train, which was about to start.

"Hurry up! All aboard!" exclaimed Hynard, and, as Roy watched, he saw Tupper thrust Mr. De Royster's diamond into his own pocket.

"They're robbing him!" thought the boy from the ranch. "I must warn him!"

He started forward. Mortimer De Royster grabbed up his suit-case and started for the train. Then he became aware that Mr. Baker had not handed him back his watch, while the other man had his pin.

"My timepiece!" he exclaimed. "I'll show it to you when we get in the train. I assure you it's a very fine one. And my pin—I would not like to lose it! Give them back!"

Hardly had he spoken when Hynard thrust his hand down

Frank V. Webster

into the inside pocket of Mr. De Royster's coat. His object was to grab his pocketbook, the bulging outline of which he had seen.

"Look out!" cried Roy in a loud voice, springing from his hiding place. "Look out! They're swindlers! They've got your watch and pin, and they're trying to get your money!"

"There's that boy!" exclaimed Hynard, as he drew out his hand.

But Mr. De Royster had felt the sneaking fingers, and had made a grab for them. He was too late, however, and, in attempting to catch Hynard he stumbled and fell.

"Come on!" cried Baker to his companions. "Let him go! We've got the stuff."

"Grab them!" cried Roy to De Royster. "I'll help you."

He rushed forward. No sooner did the swindlers see him coming, than they changed their plans. They had intended jumping on the train, which was already in motion, and leaving Mr. De Royster behind, after they had his watch and diamond.

But Roy's quickness prevented this. Baker signalled to his companions, and they ran off down the track.

"Come on!" cried Roy. "We'll catch them!"

"No! I must go to New York," replied the salesman as he arose, and brushed off his clothes. "The train is going."

"But they've got your valuables!"

"I know it. I was a fool, but it's too late now. Help me aboard."

The train was gathering headway. Roy ceased his pursuit of the robbers and helped De Royster aboard, the young man carrying his dress-suit case. Then Roy followed, while the four swindlers kept on down the railroad tracks.

Frank V. Webster

CHAPTER X

ROY GAINS A FRIEND

"Come neah gettin' left, sah!" exclaimed the colored porter of Roy's car, as our hero, followed by Mortimer De Royster, entered the coach. "Dat were a close call, sah."

"Yes, but I wish I had had a chance to round-up those swindlers. I'd shown them how we handle such chaps out on the ranch!" exclaimed Roy.

"Swindlers? Was dem nicely dressed gen'men swindlers?" inquired the porter.

"Swindlers, upon my word, they are the very worst kind," put in De Royster. "The idea of tricking me into letting them see my watch, and then keeping it, don't you know! I shall report them to the authorities."

"I'm afraid it will not do much good," remarked Roy. "They are far enough away by now, and we're getting farther off from them every minute."

"That's so. Well, then, my watch and diamond pin are gone," and the dude seemed to accept the loss quite calmly.

"Excuse me, sah," broke in the colored man, addressing De Royster, "but has youh a ticket for dis parlor car?"

"Not yet. I could not buy one at the little station back there, but you may get me one, from the conductor, don't you know," spoke the well-dressed youth, taking a roll of bills from his pocket. At the sight of the money the eyes of the colored man shone in anticipation of a tip he might receive. His opinion of the stranger went up several points. Such is the effect of money, and it is not always the right one.

"Are you going to travel in this car?" asked Roy.

"Yes, it looks like a fairly decent coach. I am really quite particular how I ride."

Roy was rather amused at the airs Mortimer De Royster assumed, and he did not quite know whether to like him or not. The youth had an affected manner of speaking, and some oddities, but, in spite of these Roy thought he might be all right at heart.

The boy from the ranch had learned, from his life in the west, not to judge persons by outward appearances, though they often give an indication of character.

"I don't believe I thanked you for what you did for me," went on De Royster to Roy, when the porter returned with his ticket and the change. The colored man's heart was made happy by a generous tip.

"I don't know that I did anything in particular. I didn't think they were going to take your hide off, or I would have warned you sooner."

"My hide off? I don't quite catch your meaning, my dear

chap—Oh, yes, I see. You mean they were going to skin me. Oh, yes. That's a good joke. Ha! Ha! Well, thanks to you, they didn't."

"Still they got something."

"Yes, that watch was a valuable one, and one my father gave me as a present. The diamond was worth considerable, too. But I am glad they did not get my money. Only for your timely warning they might have. Some of it is mine, but the most of it belongs to the firm I work for."

"They tried to get me into some swindling games, but I refused to have anything to do with them," and Roy told of the efforts of Baker and his cronies.

"I was easily taken in," admitted Mortimer De Royster. "I am ashamed of myself."

"Do you carry a valuable stock?" asked Roy, wondering if it were not dangerous to have so much jewelry about one.

"Quite valuable, yes, but all traveling jewelry salesmen belong to a league, and if thieves get away with anything belonging to any member, we have the services of a good detective agency to run the criminals down. The professional thieves know this, and, as capture is almost certain in the end, we have little fear of being robbed. These swindlers took my personal property, and nothing belonging to the firm, I'm glad to say."

"Perhaps you will get it back," suggested Roy.

"No, I'm afraid not. But I say, my dear chap, where are you going? You don't look as if you had traveled much."

"I haven't. I am going to New York on business for my father."

"To New York? Good! Then I shall have company on the way. That is unless you don't like to be seen with one who lets himself be robbed so easily."

"That would not make any difference to me."

"Thank you. Perhaps I may be able to be of some service to you in New York. I know the town fairly well."

"That will be very kind of you. I know nothing about it, and I'm afraid I'll be rather green when I get there. I have lived on a ranch all my life."

"On a ranch? Fancy now! Really, don't you know, I often used to think I would like to be a cowboy," drawled the dude.

Roy looked at the slim figure, and delicate features of Mr. De Royster, and thought that he would hardly be strong enough for the rough life on the plains. But he was too polite to mention this.

"Yes," went on the well-dressed youth, "if I had not gone into the jewelry business I might now be a 'cow-puncher,'—I believe that is what you call those gentlemen who take charge of wild steers?" and he looked at his companion inquiringly.

"Yes, some folks call 'em that."

"It must be a very nice sort of life. Now this sort of thing is rather tame, don't you know."

"Well, you had it exciting enough a while ago."

"So I did," admitted Mr. De Royster with a smile. "But that doesn't happen every day. I wish I could do you some favor, in return for what you did for me."

"I didn't do much. I wish I could have gotten them in time to have saved your watch and chain. But they stampeded before I could rope them."

"Stampeded?"

"Yes, I mean they started to run."

"Oh, yes. And—er—rope—"

"Oh, I forgot you didn't understand my lingo. I meant catch them. Whenever we want to catch anything on the ranch, we rope it. Throw a lariat over it, you know."

"Oh, yes, a lasso. I should like to have seen you lasso those chaps. Have you a lasso with you?"

"I have one in my large valise."

"Where are you going to stop in New York?"

"I don't know yet. I'm going to look around for a good place to get my grub, and a bunk after I get there."

"Your grub and bunk?" Mr. De Royster seemed puzzled.

"Well, I mean my meals and a place to sleep."

"Ah, then perhaps I can be of service to you. I know most of the best hotels, and I can introduce you to the managers of some of them. Do you intend to remain in the city long?"

"I can't tell. I don't just know how long my father's business will keep me. Probably I shall be there several weeks."

"Then I'll tell you what I'll do," said De Royster, in a friendly tone. "I'll get you fixed up at a good hotel, and then I'll show you the sights."

"But how can you spare the time from your business?" asked Roy, who was beginning to think he had found a real friend in the rather eccentric person of Mortimer De Royster.

"Oh, my work is nearly done now for the season. I shall not start out on the road again until fall, when I shall take goods for the spring trade. I was selling Christmas stock this trip."

"Christmas stock, and it is only June," exclaimed Roy. "My, but they hustle things in the East!"

"They have to. That's why I'll have some spare time now. I can show you various sights of interest, and, in turn, you must promise to protect me from robbers. I think I'll have to get a guardian if this keeps on," and the dude laughed at his joke.

"I'll do my best," replied Roy. "If I see those fellows again, they'll not get off so easily."

"Then we'll consider ourselves friends!" exclaimed De Royster, extending his hand, which Roy shook warmly.

The boy was quite attracted to the young man, whom he began to like more and more, as he saw that, under his queer ways, he hid a heart of real worth and kindness.

CHAPTER XI

ROY STOPS A RUNAWAY

With a companion who proved himself as interesting as did Mortimer De Royster, the time passed very quickly for Roy. Almost before he knew it the train was pulling into Chicago, where they changed cars.

He wanted to stop off and view the stock yards, but there was not time for this. However he saw much of interest from the car windows, and De Royster pointed out various objects, explaining them as the express passed by.

"We'll soon be in New York now," said the well-dressed youth, as the train passed beyond the confines of the "Windy City."

"Is New York larger than Chicago?" asked Roy.

"Larger? Well, I guess, and it beats it every way."

"What's that you said, young man?" inquired an individual, seated back of Roy and his new friend.

"I said New York was larger and better in every way than Chicago, don't you know," replied De Royster, looking at the man through his single eyeglass.

"You must hail from New York then?"

"I do."

"I thought so. You don't know Chicago, or you wouldn't say that. Chicago has New York beaten any way you look at it."

"Then I reckon you're from Chicago, stranger," put in Roy, who had the easy and familiar manners which life in the west breeds.

"I am, and I don't believe I'm far wrong when I say you're from off a ranch."

"I am," admitted Roy, wondering how the stranger had guessed so soon.

"Well, there's no use getting into a dispute over our respective cities," went on the stranger. "Everyone thinks his home town is the best. Are you two traveling far?"

Thus the conversation opened, and the three were soon chatting pleasantly together.

In due time the train arrived at Jersey City, just across the Hudson River from New York.

"Here we are!" exclaimed Mr. De Royster. "A short trip across the ferry now, and we'll be in the biggest city in the Western hemisphere."

Roy followed his friend from the train, mingling with the crowd on the platform under the big shed.

"Wait a minute!" exclaimed Roy.

"What for?"

"I've got to see about my baggage. It's checked. I wonder if I can hire a pack mule, or get a stage driver to bring it up?"

"Pack mule?"

"Sure. That's how I got it from the ranch to the depot."

Mortimer De Royster laughed.

"I guess there isn't a pack mule within two thousand miles of here," he said. "Nor a stage either, unless it's the automobile ones on Fifth avenue. But I'll show you what to do. Wait a minute though. You don't know where you're going to stop, do you?"

"Not exactly."

"Then if you'll allow me, I'll pick out a good hotel for you."

"I'll leave it to you, pardner," said Roy, with a helpless feeling that, however much he might know about ranch life, he was all at sea in a big city.

"All right. Then I'll give your checks to an expressman, and he'll bring the trunks to the hotel. Right over this way."

Mortimer De Royster led Roy through the crowd, to the express office. The matter of the baggage was soon attended to, and the agent promised to have the trunk and large valise at the hotel before night. It was now four o'clock.

"Come on!" cried De Royster again, pushing his way through

the crowd, with Roy who carried a small valise, containing a few clothes, following close after him.

"Wait a minute!" again called the boy from the ranch.

"What's the matter now?"

"I want to sort of get my bearings. This is a new trail to me, and I'd like to get the lay of the land. Say, what's all the stampede about? These folks are milling, ain't they?"

"Stampede? This isn't a stampede. They're in a rush to get the ferry boat. What do you mean by milling?"

"Why they're like cattle going around and around, and they don't seem to be getting anywhere."

"Oh, that's it, eh, my dear chap. Well, they're all anxious to get to New York, that's why they're rushing so. Come on or we'll miss the boat."

Mortimer De Royster led the way through the ferry house, and out on the boat. He took a seat in the ladies' cabin, and Roy sat down beside him. The dude had bought a paper, which he was glancing over, momentarily paying no attention to Roy.

Suddenly the boy from the ranch, who was looking about him with curious eyes, jumped up and exclaimed:

"Something's the matter. The depot has been cut loose!"

"Cut loose? What do you mean?"

"Why, we're afloat! There's water outside."

"Of course, my dear fellow. We're on the ferry boat, crossing to New York. What did yew think?"

"Are we on a boat?"

"Certainly. Where did you think you were?"

"I thought we were in the depot room, waiting for the boat to come in."

"Why, no. This is the boat. But of course the approach to it is through the depot, and it is hard to tell exactly where the dock leaves off and the boat begins. I should have told you, but I got interested in the paper."

"I was a little startled at first," admitted Roy with a smile. "I thought something had happened."

Several passengers who had heard this exclamation, were also smiling, but Roy did not mind this. Everything was so strange and novel that he wanted to see it all at once. It was no wonder that he mistook the boat for the waiting room of the station, as the ferry boat was so broad, and the cabin so large, that often strangers are deceived that way.

De Royster soon took Roy out on the lower deck, and showed him New York, lying across the Hudson river, the sky-scrapers towering above the water line, the various boats plying to and fro, and the great harbor.

"It's wonderful! Wonderful!" exclaimed the boy from the ranch. "It's different from what I expected. I never even dreamed New York was like this."

"Wait; you haven't begun to see it."

And, a little later, when they landed, and were crossing West street, with its congested traffic, Roy began to think his companion was right.

For a moment the noise and excitement confused the boy. There were two long lines of vehicles, mostly great trucks and drays, going up and down, for West street is on the water front, adjoining the docks where the steamships come in, and the wagons cart goods to and from them.

Then there was a big throng of people, hurrying to and from the ferries, several of which came in close together. The people all seemed in a rush, a trait, which Roy was soon to discover, affected nearly every one in New York. He saw policemen standing on the crossings, and, whenever the officer held up his hand, the travel of the vehicles stopped as if by magic, leaving a lane for pedestrians to cross.

"He's got them pretty well trained," observed Roy.

"Yes, he belongs to the traffic squad. Any driver who refused to do as the officer says, will be arrested. But come on. I want to take you to your hotel."

Trying to see everything at once, Roy followed his new friend. Suddenly, as he was in the midst of a press of wagons, men and women, in the middle of the street, he heard a cry:

"Runaway! Runaway! Horse is coming! Look out!"

Instantly the policeman began shoving people to one side, to get them out of the path of the runaway. Truck drivers began pulling their steeds to either curb. Roy looked down the street and saw a horse, attached to a cab, coming on at a gallop. Thanks to the prompt action of other drivers the

Frank V. Webster

runaway had a clear field.

"Look out!" shouted the officer. "Hey there, young man!" to Roy. "Git out of the street!"

But Roy had other intentions. He handed his valise to De Royster, who was vainly pulling him by the arm.

"Come on out of here!" cried De Royster. "You'll get run over."

"Take my satchel," said Roy.

"What are you going to do?"

"I'm going to stop that horse!"

"You'll be killed!"

"Say, I guess I know how to handle horses. It won't be the first one I've caught!"

Mortimer De Royster, giving one more look at the maddened animal, which was now close at hand, made a leap for the sidewalk. Roy looked up, gauged the distance, and, to his horror saw that the cab contained a lady and a little girl. There was no driver on the seat.

"Look out! You'll be killed!" shouted several in the crowd.

"The boy's crazy!" muttered the policeman He took a step forward, as if to drag Roy out of the way.

The next instant the boy had made a leap, just as the horse reached him. It was a leap to one side, but not to get out of the way. It was only to escape the flying hoofs, for, an instant later, Roy had the plunging horse by the bridle, and was hanging on for dear life.

Frank V. Webster

CHAPTER XII

AT THE HOTEL

There were confused shouts from the crowd. Several men rushed forward, in spite of the efforts of the officer to hold them back. Women screamed, and several fainted.

The horse was rearing and kicking, but Roy, plucky lad that he was, held on like grim death.

With one hand firmly grasping the bridle, he reached up with the other, and clasped the nostrils of the horse in a tight grip. This served to prevent the horse from breathing well, and, as his lungs needed plenty of air, on account of his fast run, the animal probably concluded he had met his master.

"That's right! Hold him!" called a man. "I'll help you in a minute!"

"I guess I can manage him now," said Roy calmly. "There now, old fellow," he went on, speaking soothingly to the horse. The animal was having hard work to breathe. Roy saw this and loosened his hold slightly. Then he began to pat the horse, continuing to speak to it. The animal, which was more frightened than vicious, began to calm down.

"I've got him!" exclaimed the policeman, coming up and taking hold of the bridle.

"Oh, he's all right now; aren't you, old fellow?" spoke Roy, as he rubbed the horse's muzzle.

Indeed the animal did seem to be. His dangerous hoofs were still, and, though he trembled a bit, he was quieting down.

"That was a fine catch, my lad," remarked one man. "Where did you learn to stop runaway horses?"

"Out on my father's ranch in Colorado. This is nothing. We have a runaway every day out there. I've often caught 'em."

"Then the city ought to hire a few lads like you to give some of our policemen lessons," went on the man, with a meaning glance at the officer.

"Come now, move on. Don't collect a crowd," spoke the bluecoat gruffly. He was a little bit ashamed that he had not made an attempt to stop the horse, but it was due more to thoughtlessness than to actual fear. Besides, he first considered getting the women out of harm's way.

"It was a brave act," went on the man. "I'd like to shake hands with you, young man."

He extended his hand which Roy, blushing at the praise, accepted.

"Here, I want to get in on that," exclaimed another man, and soon as many as could crowd around Roy were shaking hands with him, while murmurs of admiration were heard on all sides.

Frank V. Webster

Meanwhile the lady in the cab was being assisted out by a gentleman. Then she took her little girl in her arms. The child spoke, in a high clear voice, that could be heard above the noise of traffic, which had started up again, when it was seen that the runaway was stopped.

"Mother, is that the boy who caught the naughty horsie?"

"Yes, dear, mother wants to thank him."

"So do I, mother. And I want to kiss him for stopping the bad horsie that scared Mary."

There was a laugh at this, and Roy blushed deeper than ever.

"Come on," he said to Mortimer De Royster, who had made his way to his side. "Let's get out of this. Anybody would think I was giving a Wild-West exhibition."

"Well, that's pretty near what it was. I never saw a runaway better stopped, and I've seen some of our best policemen try it. You certainly know how to manage horses."

"Even if I don't know when I'm on a ferry boat," added Roy with a laugh. "But it would be a wonder if I didn't know something about cattle. I've been among 'em all my life."

"Excuse me, sir," spoke the lady who had been in the cab. "I want to thank you for what you did," and she extended her hand, encased in a neat glove.

Roy instinctively held out his hand, and then he drew it back. He noted that it was covered with foam and mud, where the horse had splashed it up on the bridle which he grasped. He had not noticed this when the men congratulated him. The lady saw his hesitation and exclaimed:

"What? You hesitate on account of not wanting to soil my gloves? There!" and before Roy could stop her she had grasped both his hands in her own, practically ruining her new gloves, for his left hand was more dirty than was his right. "What do I care for my gloves?" she exclaimed.

"Can't I kiss the nice boy, mother?" pleaded the little girl, whom her parent had placed on the crosswalk, close beside her.

There was another laugh, but Roy was not going to mind that. Though he had no brothers or sisters, he was very fond of children. The next instant he had stooped over and kissed the little girl.

Once more the crowd laughed, but in a friendly way, for Roy was a lad after the heart of every New Yorker—brave, fearless, yet kind.

"I can't begin to thank you," went on the lady. "But for you, Mary and I might have been killed."

"Oh, I guess the horse would have slowed up pretty soon, ma'am," replied Roy.

"Now don't make light of it," urged the lady. "I wish you would call at my home, and see us. My husband will want to add his thanks to mine. Here is our address."

She gave Roy a card on which was engraved the name, "Mrs. Jonathan Rynear," and the address was uptown in New York.

"The horse took fright when the cabman got down to get something for me in a store," she said, "and ran away before any one could stop him. I can drive horses, but I could not reach the reins of this one, and I dared not let go of my little girl. Now I want you to be sure and come. Will you?"

"Yes, ma'am," spoke Roy, and then, when Mrs. Rynear had shaken hands with him again, Roy managed to make his way through the crowd, and, accompanied by De Royster, he started up the street.

"Well, your entrance to New York is rather theatrical," observed Mortimer De Royster. "You'll get into the papers, first thing you know, really you will, my dear fellow."

"That's just where I don't want to get," said Roy quickly, as he thought that his mission might not be so well accomplished, if Mr. Annister read of the arrival in New York, of the son of the man whose agent he was. "How can it get in the papers?"

"Why, the reporters are all over New York. They'll hear of this in some way, or the policeman will tell them. Besides, the policeman has to report all such happenings on his post, and the reporters to go to the police station in search of news."

"But how will they know I did it?"

"That's so. I don't believe they will, old chap. You didn't give the lady your name."

"No, and I'm glad of it."

"Why; don't you want any one to know you're in New York?"

"Well, not right away. I have certain reasons for it. Later it may make no difference. But I guess the reporters are not liable to know it was me."

"No, perhaps not. The policeman may claim the credit of stopping the runaway. Some of 'em do, so as to get promotion more quickly."

"It wasn't much of a job to stop that runaway."

"Wasn't it? Well, it looked so to me, and I guess it did to the rest of the crowd. But you're all mud. The horse must have splashed you. However you'll soon be at your hotel. We'll take a train."

Still quite bewildered by the noise and confusion Roy followed De Royster up a flight of steps, not knowing where he was going. The next he knew was that his friend had dropped two tickets into the box of the elevated station, and they were waiting for an uptown train. Presently it came along, making the station and track rock and sway with the vibration.

"Come on," cried De Royster.

"Where are you going?" asked Roy, hanging back.

"On the elevated train, of course."

"It isn't safe!" exclaimed the boy from the ranch. "It is shaking now. It'll topple down! It needs bracing! Do you mean to tell me they run trains up in the air, on a track, and they don't fall off?"

"Of course. Come on. It's safe, even if it does shake a bit. It always does. There's no danger of it falling off. Next time we'll take the subway."

"All aboard! Step lively!" cried the guard at the gate, and Roy, with some misgivings, followed his friend.

Frank V. Webster

The ride, on a level with the second-story windows of the buildings, was a great novelty to the boy from the ranch and he soon got over his feeling of nervousness in looking out at the strange sights on every hand.

"Here we are!" exclaimed De Royster at length. "I'll take you to the hotel."

They got out, walked down a flight of steps, and soon were in front of a good, though not showy hotel. In spite of the fact that it was not one of the most fashionable in New York, the magnificence of the entrance, with its rich hangings, the marble ornamentation, the electric lights and the stained glass, made Roy wonder if his friend had not made some mistake. It seemed more like the home of some millionaire, than a public hotel.

"Go ahead; I'll be right with you," called De Royster, as he showed Roy into the lobby. "I want to speak to a gentleman a moment."

Somewhat bewildered, Roy advanced into the middle of the lobby, with its marble floor. Though he was not aware of it, he made rather a queer figure, with his clothes of unstylish cut, his travel-stained appearance, the mud on his hands and garments, and his general air of being a stranger, totally unused to New York ways.

"Well, what do you want?" suddenly exclaimed the voice of a boy in a uniform that seemed to consist of nothing but brass buttons. "We don't allow peddlers in here!"

CHAPTER XIII

A VISIT TO MR. ANNISTER

Roy turned and looked at the boy who had made the somewhat insulting remark.

"I beg your pardon, stranger," he replied in his western drawl. "I didn't quite catch your remark."

"Aw, come off!" slangily replied the brass-buttoned boy, one of many in the hotel employed to show guests to their rooms whenever summoned by a bell rung by the clerk. "What are you, anyhow? Selling patent medicine or some Indian cure?" For Roy plainly showed the effect of his western life, his hair being a little longer than it is worn in the east, his clothes rather too large for him, and his broad-brimmed hat quite conspicuous.

"So you think I'm rustling medicine, eh?" he asked the boy.

"I don't know what you're 'rustling' but I know if you try to sell anything in this joint, you'll get the poke, see!"

Roy began to think the language of the East was almost as effective as that of the West in expressing ideas.

"I'm not selling medicine, stranger," Roy went on, using the term he had picked up among the cowboys when they meet one whom they do not know. "I'm going to put up at this bunk-house, I reckon."

"That's a good one!" exclaimed the boy with a laugh. "What Wild West show are you from? This is no theatrical boarding house. Better beat it out of here before the clerk sees you."

But the talk between the two boys had been overheard by the clerk, who, in a hotel, holds authority next to the owner.

"What's the trouble there, Number twenty-six?" he asked, addressing the bell boy.

"Aw, here's a guy what t'inks he's goin' to stay here an' sell patent medicines," replied the boy.

"What's that? Of course we don't allow any peddling schemes in the hotel. Send him out."

"I did, but he won't go."

"Your boy is mistaken, stranger," replied Roy, walking up to the desk, and looking around for Mortimer De Royster, who, it seemed, had been delayed in speaking to a friend. Several men in the hotel lobby drew near and listened with interest to what was going on. "I came here to put up at this hotel," went on Roy. "I was sent here by a friend of mine."

"We don't take theatrical people," said the clerk, stiffly.

"I'm not from a theatre. I tell you my friend sent me here. He'll be here himself in a minute."

The clerk did not look very much impressed, and Roy feared

he was going to order him out of the hotel. The boy did not want to be thus publicly put to shame.

"Who's your friend?" asked the clerk.

"Mr. Mortimer De Royster."

"Oh, that's all right!" exclaimed the clerk with a great change of manner. "Any friend of Mr. De Royster is welcome. Boy, take the gentleman's grip. What sort of a room would you like?"

The bell boy, who had thought to put Roy out of the place, was obliged much against his will to take his valise.

"That's all right," said Roy good-naturedly to the boy. "I can carry my baggage. It isn't heavy. I don't know that I'm going to stop here after all. I think—"

Just then De Royster came pushing his way through the little crowd about the desk.

"Hello, Charlie!" he exclaimed, addressing the clerk. "How are you, old chap? Looking fine, upon my word!"

"Good afternoon, Mr. De Royster," replied the clerk cordially, extending his hand. "Glad to see you. So you're back from your trip?"

"Yes, but I came pretty near not coming. Might not be alive if it wasn't for my friend, Mr. Bradner, here. By the way, I want you to give him the best in the house. He's a great friend of mine. Treat him well."

"Of course we shall. We were just going to give him a good room—er—ahem, Mr. Bradner, will you please register?"

and he swung the book around on the desk, dipping a pen in an ink bottle at the same time.

Roy hesitated, and smiled just a little. He was contrasting the treatment he might have received if Mr. De Royster had not been there.

"What's the matter?" asked the jewelry salesman, seeing that something unusual had taken place.

"Oh, nothing much," replied Roy. "They took me for a member of a Wild West show, I guess, and they were a little doubtful whether they'd let me bunk here or not."

"Ahem! All a mistake! It was the bell boy's fault," said the clerk, somewhat embarrassed.

"Here, Number twenty-six, take the gentleman's grip. Any friend of yours, Mr. De Royster, is doubly welcome here. We can give you a fine room, Mr. Bradner."

"All right," replied Roy, good naturedly. "I'll take one."

"I'll select it for you," put in Mr. De Royster, as he was in some doubt as to Roy's finances, and he did not want to take too extravagant an apartment.

Roy was soon shown to a pleasant room, Mortimer accompanying him. Every one connected with the hotel seemed anxious to aid the boy from the ranch, now that it was shown he had wealthy friends. Roy thought De Royster must be a person of some influence. He was partly right, though the influence came more from the rich and respected relatives of the young jewelry salesman, than from himself. However, it answered the same purpose.

"I am sorry you were annoyed by that clerk, my dear chap," said De Royster, when he was seated in the room he had selected for Roy. "I was unavoidably detained, speaking to a friend I met, don't you know."

"It's all right," replied Roy. "It all adds to my experience, and I expect to get a lot of it while I'm in the East."

"What are your next plans?"

"Well, I hardly know. I have certain business to do for my father, but I hardly know how to set about it."

"Perhaps I can tell you."

"I wish you could."

"If it is a secret don't tell me," said De Royster, noting that Roy hesitated.

"It is a sort of a secret mission. I'm here to round up a man, and see what sort of branding marks he has on him—that is, whether he's honest or not."

"That is a queer mission for a boy like you to be sent on."

"Perhaps, but my father had no one else. I will tell you as much as I can, and see what you have to say."

Thereupon Roy told his friend about the real estate matter, and Mr. Annister's connection with it, though he mentioned no names.

"Let me consider it a bit," said the dude, when Roy had finished. The latter began to think his friend was more capable than had at first appeared, and, in spite of his rather affected talk, could be relied upon for good advice.

"Here is what I would do, in your place," said De Royster, at length. "I would get my hair cut, order a new suit of clothes or perhaps two and appear as much as possible like a New Yorker, don't you know. You say you don't want that man to know you are here from the ranch. Well, he certainly would if you appeared before him as you are now. But, if you—er—well, we'll say 'spruce up' a bit, you can be sure he'll never connect you with the West. Then you can make whatever inquiries you like."

"That's good advice. I'll follow it. I'm much obliged to you."

"Don't mention it, my dear chap. Now, old man"—(Roy thought it was strange to be addressed as "old man")—"I've got to go. I'll leave you my card, and address, and, if you get into trouble, why, telephone or call on me. Now, good luck."

He shook hands with Roy and left. The boy from the ranch was a little lonesome after De Royster had gone, but he knew he would from now on, very probably have to rely on himself, and he decided to start in at once.

After supper he went to the hotel barber shop, and had his hair cut to the length it was worn by New Yorkers. He wanted to go out and get a new suit, but he knew the clothing stores would not be open at night.

His trunk arrived the next morning, and, having arranged his things in his room, the boy from the ranch set out to buy some new garments, following De Royster's advice.

"Well, I certainly don't look like a cowboy now," thought Roy, as he surveyed himself in the glass, after the change. "Now to call on Mr. Annister. I don't believe he'll suspect me of being on his trail."

A little later Roy was on his way down-town, having inquired from the clerk how to get to the office of the real estate agent. He was soon at the place, a big office building, in which several firms had their quarters.

He got in the express elevator, which went up at a speed that took away his breath, and was let out at the twentieth floor, where the real estate agent had his rooms.

"Is Mr. Annister in?" Roy asked the office boy.

"I don't know. What's your business?"

"My business is with Mr. Annister."

"What's your name?"

"That doesn't matter. Tell Mr. Annister I called to see him regarding the renting of some property on Bleecker street," for that was where the building was located in which Roy and his father were interested.

"All right. I'll tell him, but I don't believe he'll see you," replied the office boy, not very good-naturedly, as he went into an inner room. In a little while he returned and said:

"Walk in. He'll see you a few minutes, but he's very busy."

A few seconds later Roy stood in the presence of Caleb Annister.

CHAPTER XIV

ROY'S TRICK

"What can I do for you, sir?" asked the real estate agent as Roy entered. "Take a chair."

Caleb Annister had been a little curious to see the young man whom his office boy described. He could not imagine what was wanted, but he scented a possible customer to engage some of the offices in the structure, for which he collected the rents.

"I want to make some inquiries regarding an office in your Bleeker street building," said Roy, for such was the designation of the property in question.

"Ah, yes. You are going to open an office, perhaps?"

"I may." This was the truth as Roy's father had said, if the agent was found to be dishonest, a new one, with an office in the Bleecker street building might be engaged.

"Aren't you rather young to go in business?"

"Perhaps, but I am representing other persons. Have you any offices to rent in that building?"

"A few."

"What do they rent for?"

It was Roy's idea to make inquiries in the guise of a possible tenant, and, see what prices Mr. Annister was charging. What his next move was you shall very soon see.

"Well, young man, rents are very high in that building. It is in a good neighborhood, where property is increasing in value all the while, and we have to charge high rents. Besides there is a good demand for offices there."

This, Roy thought, was not the sort of information Mr. Annister had sent to Mr. Bradner at the ranch.

"Do you own the building?" asked the western lad, wanting to see what the agent would say.

"No, but I am in full charge. It would be no use for you to see the owner, as he leaves everything to me. He would not give you any lower rent rate than I would. Besides, he lives away out West, and never comes to New York."

"Can you give me an idea of what the rents are for such offices as are vacant?" asked Roy, trying not to let any Western expressions slip into his talk, as he wanted to pose as a New Yorker.

"Is it for yourself?"

"No, for parties I represent."

"I can give you a list of such offices as are vacant, with the prices, and you can go and see them. The janitor will show them to you, if I send him a note."

"That will do very well."

Caleb Annister went over some books, and soon handed Roy a list of room numbers, with the prices at which they rented by the month. It needed but a glance at the list, and a rapid calculation on the part of Roy, who was quick at figures, to see that if the entire building rented in the same proportion, the income from it was much larger than what his father was receiving. Clearly there was something wrong, and he must find out where it was.

"I shall look at these offices," he said, "and let you know whether or not they will suit my friend."

"What is the name?" asked Mr. Annister, preparing to write a note to the janitor.

Now Roy was "up against it" as he put it. He did not want to give his name, or Mr. Annister would suspect something at once, and, possibly, put some obstacles in his way. Nor did he want to tell an untruth, and give a false name. Finally he saw a way out of the difficulty.

He decided to give De Royster's name, as he had an idea that if Mr. Annister proved to be dishonest, as it seemed he was, the young jewelry salesman could be induced to take the agency of the building, at least until he had to begin his travels again. To do this De Royster would need an office in the building, so it would be no untruth for Roy to give his name, and say he was looking for apartments for him. He knew his friend would consent. So he said:

"You may make out the note in the name of Mortimer De Royster."

"De Royster? That is a good name. I know some of

the family."

Mr. Annister wrote the note, and gave it to Roy, not asking his name. In fact, the real estate man took his caller to be an office boy for Mr. De Royster, for business men in New York frequently send their office helpers on errands of importance, and this was no more than the average office boy could do.

With the note Roy went to the Bleecker Building, as it was called. He found the janitor, who readily showed him the vacant offices.

"Aren't rents rather high here?" asked Roy.

"That's what they are. But this is a good location for business men, and they're willing to pay for it," answered the man.

"Have you no cheaper offices than these?"

"No. In fact all the others cost more. Some men have several rooms, and they pay a good price."

"How many offices, or sets of offices, have you in this building? I should think it would keep you busy looking after them."

"It does," replied the janitor, who, like others of his class, liked a chance to complain of how hard they worked. "There are more than a hundred offices in this building."

"And are most of them rented?"

"All but the five I showed you. I tell you the man who owns this building has a fine thing out of it. He must make a lot over his expenses."

"Who owns it?" asked Roy, wanting to see how much the janitor knew.

"I couldn't tell you. Mr. Annister never told me. He hires me. I guess he must have an interest in the property."

"Yes, entirely too much of an interest in it," thought Roy. "He has some of my interest, and I'm going to get it back."

There was one thing more he wanted to know.

"Are the tenants good pay?" he asked.

"They have to be, young man. If they get behind a month Mr. Annister puts them out. That's why those five offices are vacant. But they'll soon be rented. You'd better hurry if you want one."

"My friend will think it over," answered the boy from the ranch.

He had found out what he wanted to know. The property, instead of decreasing in value as Mr. Annister had said, was increasing. Nearly every office was rented at a good price, and the tenants were prompt pay, save in a few instances. It did not require much calculation to see that the income from the property was nearly double what Mr. Annister reported it to be to Mr. Bradner. That meant but one thing. The dishonest agent was keeping part of the rent for himself, and sending false reports to Roy's father.

But it was one thing to know this, and another to prove it. Roy left the building, thanking the janitor for his trouble, and started back toward Mr. Annister's office.

"I wonder what I had better do?" he thought.

CHAPTER XV

CALEB ANNISTER IS SURPRISED

Perhaps, if Mr. Bradner had known just the extent of the rascality of his agent, he might not have sent Roy to investigate. But, at the worst, he only imagined that perhaps the man might be careless in collecting the rents, which would account for the small income from the property.

Roy certainly had a difficult task before him, and he hardly knew how to undertake it. Should he confront Caleb Annister with the evidence of his dishonesty, or would it be better to wait a while? He had all the proof he needed; but what would be the outcome? That was what puzzled Roy.

Finally, with a decision characteristic of him, and following his nature, which was influenced by the openness of action associated with the West, he made up his mind.

"I'll go right back and see him," reasoned the boy, "tell him who I am, show him that I know he's been cheating us, and demand that he make good the money he has taken. Then I'll see how he acts. If he pays back the rent money he has retained I guess dad will not be hard on him. If he doesn't—"

Roy knew his father was a man who would have his rights if

there was any way of getting them. He had half a notion to telegraph his father for instructions, but he wanted to do the work all alone, if he could.

When he got back to the office where Mr. Annister had his rooms, the boy in the outer apartment did not stop Roy to ask him his business. He at once announced him to the agent, who told Roy to come in. The boy from the ranch nerved himself for what was coming. He felt just as he used to when, for the first time, he mounted a new bucking bronco. There was no telling just what the animal would do. Likewise he did not know how Caleb Annister would act when he exposed his rascality.

"Well, did you see the offices?" asked the real estate man.

"Yes, sir."

"Did you like them? We think they are the best in New York."

"They are very fine. The rents are higher than I thought to find them."

"Perhaps, but you must know there is a good demand for offices in that neighborhood. I could have rented them several times, since they were vacant, but I wanted to get good tenants, who would pay."

"You have no cheaper offices you could let Mr. De Royster have?"

"None. In fact I am thinking of raising the rents of those."

Roy wondered if he and his father would get any of the increase.

"That property must be quite valuable," he went on.

"It is."

Roy now felt that the real estate agent had convicted himself. There was need of no further evidence. It was time to make the disclosure.

"Mr. Annister," said Roy. "Perhaps I had better introduce myself. Here is my card."

He handed over one on which he had written his name, and the address of his father's ranch, as well as that of the hotel where he was stopping.

For a moment the agent did not know what to do, as he looked at the bit of pasteboard. His face became pale, then red, then pale again. Next he smiled, in a sickly sort of way.

"So you are Roy Bradner, son of James Bradner, eh?" he asked, slowly.

"Yes, sir."

"Well, that's—that's a pretty good joke," went on the agent. "A pretty good joke."

Roy could not quite see it.

"You come East here, and pretend to want an office in the building your father owns, and you take me in completely. That is a good joke. But I see what you are after."

"That will save a lot of explanation then, Mr. Annister."

"I see what you want," the agent went on. "You wanted to

find out in a quiet way, if I was properly looking after your father's property. So you come here, and don't let me know who you are. It's a good joke. But I guess you found I was looking after your interests; didn't you? You found me faithful to my trust. Now you can go back and tell your father that I am looking well after his affairs. That's what you can do. When are you going back?"

"I don't know!" exclaimed Roy boldly, "but when I do go back I will tell my father that you are a swindler, and that you are cheating him—and me also—out of our rent money."

"What's that?" cried Mr. Annister, his face fairly purple with rage. "You dare call me a swindler! I'll have you arrested for insulting me! Leave my office at once! How dare you address me in that manner?"

"I dare because I'm right," replied Roy coolly. "You can't bluff me, Mr. Annister. I see through your game. I now demand that you pay back all the money you have retained, or I shall make a complaint against you."

The bold and fearless bearing of the boy had its effect on the real estate agent. He saw he had to deal with a lad, who, if he had had no previous business experience, was capable of looking after his own interests.

"Perhaps you will kindly explain," said the agent, in a tone he meant to be sarcastic, but which did not deceive Roy.

"Certainly. I accuse you of charging high rents for the offices in the Bleecker Building, and with sending my father only about half of what you collect!"

"Oh! So that's the game; is it?" asked the agent, with a sneer. "Perhaps you know how much I take in as rent for the offices in that building?"

"I can pretty nearly figure it out," and Roy mentioned a sum that was so near the mark that Mr. Annister was startled.

"And perhaps you know what the expenses are, the taxes, the water rent, the insurance and so forth?"

"No, but I know what you charged my father for those items, and, taking them out, at your figures, and also your commission, it would leave a larger sum than we ever received."

Mr. Annister saw that he was dealing with no novice, even if the lad was from the western ranch. He resolved to proceed on a different plan.

"You may think yourself very smart," he said to Roy, "but you do not understand New York real estate."

"I understand enough for this case, I think."

"I'm afraid not," and the agent smiled. He was beginning to get command of his nerves. "You see there are many expenses you do not know of."

"You never mentioned them to my father."

"No, I could not. Besides, how do I know that your father sent you to make these inquiries? I do not even know you are Roy Bradner. You may be an impostor."

"I think I can soon prove to you who I am. As for my authority, there is a letter from my father to you, instructing you to turn this business over to me at my demand."

He handed Mr. Annister a letter to this effect written by Mr.

Bradner, and properly executed before a notary public. The rascally agent knew the signature of Mr. Bradner only too well.

But he was not going to give up so easily.

"Any one can write a letter, and forge a signature," he said.

"Then you think I forged my father's name?" and a dangerous look came into Roy's eyes. It was a look such as that when he stopped the runaway horse.

"I don't care to have any further conversation with you," said Mr. Annister, sneeringly. "I do not recognize your authority. How do I know you are Roy Bradner? You will have to bring me better proof than this. Besides, even if you are who you say you are, that does not say you understand this renting business. It is very complicated. There are many charges I have to meet which makes the amounts received for rent much less than you have figured. Besides, the property is in bad shape, it needs repairs, and it is going down in value."

"You said a little while ago that it was increasing."

The agent started. He saw he had made a mistake.

"Oh, well," he said impatiently. "You are only a boy; you can't understand it."

"I may be only a boy, but I think I understand what is going on, and that is that you are cheating my father and me. I was in the building to-day. It is in excellent repair."

"Don't you dare accuse me of cheating!" exclaimed Mr. Annister, but his tone was not as blustering as it had been.

"I believe that is the truth."

"What do you intend to do?" inquired the agent, as he saw that Roy was firm. "Not that it makes any difference to me, for I shall communicate with your father, but I do not want you to come here and annoy me."

He was beginning to be afraid of what Roy might disclose.

"I intend to make you return the money you have unlawfully retained. I believe it is called embezzling, and is a criminal offense. But I will give you a little time. I shall call here a week from to-day. If, by that time, you do not have what I consider a proper sum ready to send to my father I shall consult with the police."

"Pooh! The police will never interfere. This is a civil matter—not criminal."

"I think it is criminal. But I will wait one week. In the meanwhile I shall write to my father and see what he advises me to do. But I shall report all the facts in the case."

"Get out of my office!" exclaimed the now angry and frightened real estate agent. "I believe you are an impostor. If you annoy me again I shall have you arrested!"

"I'll leave your office, because I have finished my business with you, and not because I am afraid of arrest," answered Roy coolly. "You know I am not an impostor. I can prove who I am. I shall call on you again in a week," and he went out in time to surprise the office boy with his ear at the key hole, listening to what was going on.

"Cracky!" exclaimed the little lad, when Roy had gone out. "He certainly talked to the boss like a Dutch Uncle."

Frank V. Webster

Meanwhile Mr. Annister sat in his office chair, much disturbed in his mind. He was in great alarm, for he knew Roy was no impostor.

"What am I going to do?" he asked himself. "He has found me out!"

He sat biting his nails nervously, his eyes roving about his office, as if seeking some way of escape from the trouble he was in. Suddenly an idea came to him.

"I must get that boy out of the way," he said in a low whisper, which even the office lad could not hear. "He knows too much. He is too smart. And I must act promptly. If I can get him out of the way for two weeks, and before he has a chance to hear from his father, the property will be mine, and I can defy them all. That's what I'll do. I'll get him out of the way!"

CHAPTER XVI

SOME NEW EXPERIENCES

Roy passed out through the outer rooms of Caleb Annister's suite of offices. He noted the eavesdropping act of the boy, but said nothing to the small chap, who seemed much embarrassed. Then Roy, with his head somewhat in a whirl over what he had just gone through, went into the tiled corridor.

He got into an elevator, but, no sooner had the attendant closed the iron-grilled door than the car seemed to fall to the bottom of the elevator well with a sickening suddenness.

"Look out!" cried the boy from the ranch, startled out of his reverie concerning Mr. Annister, by the fear that the car had broken from the cable. "She's going to smash!" he cried.

Down, down, down fell the car, but, to Roy's surprise no one seemed to mind it. To him it felt, as he expressed it, "as if the bottom had dropped out of his stomach."

Roy clung to one side of the iron grating which formed the car. Every moment he expected the cage to be dashed to pieces. Then some one laughed. Roy knew something was going on that he didn't understand.

Frank V. Webster

A moment later the car came to a gradual stop, amid a hissing of air.

"Say, stranger, does it often break loose and go on a stampede that way?" asked Roy of the attendant who opened the door at the ground floor.

"What's the matter? Did it scare you?"

"Well, it was a pretty good imitation of it," replied Roy, while the other passengers broke into laughter. "I sure thought I was going to China. What was the matter?"

"Nothing. This is an express elevator, and it drops from the twentieth story to the ground in about fifteen seconds. It lands into an air chamber, as soft as a piece of rubber. There's no danger. I do it a hundred times a day."

"You'll have to excuse me the next time," said Roy, with a smile as he got out. "I don't exactly cotton to elevators anyhow, but when they drop you like a steer falling over a cliff, why it'll be walk the stairs for mine, after this. It sure will."

"Guess you're from out West, ain't you?"

"That's what I am, and it's a mighty good place. Say, that trip sure made me dizzy."

Indeed there is a curious feeling about being dropped twenty stories in a swift elevator, and Roy might well be excused for his sensation.

However, he soon recovered himself, and, as it was noon time, and he had a good appetite, he looked about for a place to get something to eat.

He noticed a small restaurant nearby, and went in.

Instead of seeing tables set out in the place, he beheld rows of chairs, with one arm made very large, so that it served as a shelf on which to place plates, cups and saucers. In fact it was a chair and table combined.

He saw men eating, and others hurrying to and fro, so he took a vacant place, and sat there, expecting a waiter to come to him and take his order. He remained there for some time, noting that the men seated in a row on either side of him, were busy with their food, but no attendant came to him.

"This is queer," thought the boy. "The waiters must be terribly busy. They don't keep you waiting like this at my hotel."

Finally a man, seeing that Roy was a stranger, spoke to him, saying:

"You have to wait on yourself here."

"Wait on yourself?"

"Yes. You go up to that counter over there," pointing to it, "and take whatever you want. You'll find plates, knives, forks and so on. Then, if you want coffee, you take a cup, go to that counter, where the man stands, and he'll draw a cup for you."

"Thanks," replied Roy, proceeding to put these directions into use. Then for the first time he noticed that the other patrons of the restaurant were doing the same thing.

Roy helped himself to some sandwiches, crullers, a piece of cheese and some pie.

"I wonder who I pay?" he thought, as he saw no one behind the food counter to take any money. "Guess it must be the man at the coffee urn."

He carried his food to a chair, placing it on the broad arm. Then he went back for a cup of coffee.

"I got some grub back there," he said to the man. "What's the damage?"

"Pay the girl at the desk when you go out," replied the man shortly without looking around. "Tell her what you had, and she'll tell you how much it is."

"Well, isn't that the limit," exclaimed Roy, half to himself, as he got his coffee. "This is certainly a new-fangled way of getting your grub."

Still he rather liked the novelty of it. Certainly it was quick, once one learned how to go about it. Roy made a good though not very fancy meal, and then walked up to the desk, where he observed other men paying.

"Well," asked the young lady, who seemed to have a very large amount of light hair, piled up on top of her head in all sorts of waves and frizzes.

"What'd you have?"

She spoke briskly, making change for one man, and handing another one a box of cigars, that he might take one, and, all the while she never stopped chewing gum.

Roy named over the articles.

"Twenty cents!" exclaimed the girl. "Here, that's a lead

nickel!" she added quickly, to the customer just ahead of Roy. "Don't try any of them tricks on me."

Roy laid down two dimes, wondering at the cheapness of the meal, and feeling quite confused by the rush and excitement about him.

He walked out, wondering what his next move should be. He had not gone a dozen steps up the street, before he suddenly remembered that he had forgotten to mention to the young lady at the desk that he had a piece of pie.

"I've got to go right back and pay her for that pie!" thought the lad. "She'll think I'm trying to cheat her. Lucky I thought of it when I did, or they might have sent a policeman after me."

He hurried back, and made his way to the desk through a crowd of men coming out.

"Say," he began to the cashier, "I'm awfully sorry, but I made a mistake."

"No mistakes corrected after you leave the desk. See that sign?" and the girl pointed to one to that effect. "You should count your change while you're here. You can't work that game on me."

"I'm not trying to work any game," and Roy felt a little hurt that his good motive should thus be mistaken. "I had a piece of pie and I forgot to tell you of it. I came back to pay the five cents."

"Oh!"

The girl's manner changed, and she looked a little

embarrassed. "That's all right. You could have paid me to-morrow.

"But I might not be here to-morrow."

Roy laid down a five-cent piece.

"Say, but you're honest!" exclaimed the cashier, as she put back a straggling lock of her yellow hair. "You can't live in New York."

"Now I wonder why she said that?" reasoned Roy, as he walked along the street. "Can it be that every one in New York is dishonest? Well, I certainly think Mr. Annister is. I must write to father, and tell him what took place. Then I wander what I had better do next."

Roy was quite perplexed. He would have been more worried had he known what was passing through the mind of Caleb Annister at that moment.

CHAPTER XVII

CALEB ANNISTER MAKES PLANS

The rascally real estate agent was more worried over the visit of Roy than he cared to acknowledge, even to himself. The truth was that Caleb Annister was planning a bold stroke, which was nothing less than to obtain title of the building belonging to Mr. Bradner and his son.

For a long time, as Mr. Bradner had suspected, the agent had been cheating him, retaining part of the rents. But this did not satisfy Mr. Annister. He had begun to steal, and he liked that easy way of getting money so well that he determined on operations on a larger scale. Now Roy's coming was likely to interfere with this.

It was Caleb Annister's plan to obtain ownership of the building in this way. Though he had reported to Mr. Bradner that the taxes had been always paid promptly, they were, in fact, very much behind, and had not been paid for two years.

Consequently the city had put the property up for sale for unpaid taxes. A certain length of time must elapse before a title could be taken from the former owner, and given to any one who would pay the taxes and other city charges.

Mr. Annister planned to pay these back taxes without Mr. Bradner's knowledge and so become the owner of the building, which was quite valuable. But it needed about two weeks before his trick could be consummated, and with Roy on hand in New York it might not go through at all.

For the real estate agent realized, that as Roy had already begun to investigate the property, he might not stop there, but go further discover that the taxes were unpaid, and have his father pay them in the two weeks that remained, thus keeping the title of the building and land in Mr. Bradner's name.

"I must prevent that at all costs!" exclaimed the agent, as he sat in his office, when Roy had gone. "I have gone too far to back out now. And I will not be thwarted by a mere boy. Bah! Why should I be afraid of him? If I can get him out of the way—if I can have him disappear for two weeks, I can snap my fingers at him and his father too. Then I'll no longer be the agent for the Bleecker Building—I'll be the owner, and a wealthy man!"

He gave himself up to day-dreams of what this would mean. He was brought back from it, however, by the necessity of getting Roy out of the way.

"I wonder how I can do it?" he murmured.

At present Caleb Annister could see no way of bringing this about. He decided to go out for dinner, thinking, perhaps, some plan might occur to him.

As he was walking along the street he almost collided with a man who was hurrying along in the opposite direction.

"I beg your pardon!" exclaimed Mr. Annister.

"Certainly. My fault entirely," replied the other. "I—why, if it isn't Caleb Annister," he went on. "How are you?"

"Phelan Baker!" cried Mr. Annister, in a tone of surprise. "I thought you were out West."

"I was, but I arrived in New York this morning."

"And how are Sutton and Hynard?" went on Mr. Annister. "I haven't seen them since that affair of—"

"Hush! Don't mention such things in public," cautioned Mr. Baker, for what Mr. Annister referred to was a swindling game in which Baker and his cronies had been involved, and the discovery of which had made it necessary for them to leave the city awhile.

"The boys are all right," went on Mr. Baker. "Tupper is with them. In fact they came on to New York with me. We were delayed on the road." He did not say this was caused by the necessity for fleeing after robbing Mortimer De Royster. "We're at the same hotel. By the way," he went on, "you couldn't lend me fifty dollars; could you? I'm short, and the boys have very little. We haven't had any luck lately. I'd like fifty dollars for a few days. Can you let me have it?"

"I'm sorry," began Mr. Annister. "I'd like to, but the truth is I have some heavy bills to meet, and people who owe me money, have not paid me. Otherwise—"

"Well, perhaps I can get it somewhere else," said Mr. Baker. In fact he had very little hope, when he made the request of Mr. Annister, that he would get the loan. The real estate agent was known to be very "close", seldom lending money, though he was quite well off.

"I'd like to accommodate you," went on Caleb Annister, brightening up, when he saw that Mr. Baker was not going to press the matter, "but you see how it is."

"You haven't any work that you want done; have you?" asked the man who had helped to rob Mortimer De Royster, and who had tried unsuccessfully to rob and swindle Roy. "We could do almost anything you wanted done, if you paid us for it. None of us have anything in view to get a few dollars at."

Suddenly a thought came into the wicked brain of Caleb Annister. This might be the very chance he was looking for! Baker and his men could get Roy out of the way for him. He would try it.

"Perhaps you might do me a service," he said. "It is very simple, and does not amount to a great deal."

Mr. Baker knew the real estate agent well enough to feel that whenever he wanted anything done, it was no small matter. But he merely said:

"Tell me what it is. If it's possible we'll do it—for money, of course."

"Oh, it's very possible, and I will be willing to pay you and your friends well. Come and have lunch with me, and we will talk it over."

Caleb Annister had intended going to an expensive restaurant and ordering a fine meal, for he was fond of good living, but, when he found he would have to take Baker, and pay for his dinner, he changed his plans, and went to a cheap eating place.

There, sitting in a secluded corner, Mr. Annister unfolded a plot to the swindler.

"There is a certain young man, lately arrived in New York," said the real estate agent, "who is bothering me. Nothing serious, you understand, but I have a certain deal to put through and he might spoil it. I want him kept out of the way for two weeks. By that time my plans will be finished, and I don't care what he does. Do you think you can get him, and take him, say to some nearby town, or even some place in New York and keep him there for two weeks? But I must insist that no harm comes to him."

With all his swindling schemes, Mr. Annister would not go too far.

"Sure we can do it," replied Phelan Baker. "That's easy. What do we get for it?"

"If you get him away, and keep him out of sight for two weeks all will be well, and I will pay you a thousand dollars."

"Good enough! We'll do it. Now who is this boy you want taken away?"

"Roy Bradner."

"What? Roy Bradner, the boy from Triple O ranch?"

"That's the one. But what do you know of him?" and Mr. Annister was very much astonished.

"This is curious," murmured Baker. "Very curious. I'll tell you about it, Annister."

CHAPTER XVIII

ROY IN DANGER

When Roy got out into the street again, after paying for the pie he had forgotten about, he was quite puzzled as to which direction to take to get back to his hotel.

"Guess I'm off the trail," he told himself. "I'd ought to have brought a compass along. Let's see, which way is North?"

He looked about for a sight of the sun, but, though it was shining, the tall buildings hid it from view.

"Might as well be down in the grand canyon of the Colorado, as here in New York for all you can see of the sun," he murmured.

"I ought to have taken more notice of the way I came, but what with going in so many buildings, and that express elevator, I'm all turned around."

He tried to think which way to take, and then, getting over a little natural embarrassment about asking a stranger the road, he inquired of a well-dressed man the way to get to his hotel, the name of which, fortunately, Roy remembered.

"Go right down those stairs," said the man, pointing to a flight which started in a little shelter built on the sidewalk. "Take an uptown express, and you'll land right at your hotel. There's a station there."

"Station?" thought Roy. "That's a queer place for a station. Didn't have room for it above ground, I reckon."

He walked down the flight of steps, finding himself in a brilliantly lighted place. Doing as he saw the crowd do he bought a ticket at a little window and then, seeing a sign "Uptown Express Trains," he followed the throng going in that direction.

A moment later a string of cars came rumbling up along-side of the platform.

"All aboard!" called the guard.

The boy from the ranch got in and took a seat. The next moment the train started off at great speed, for it was an express, and made but few stops. Leaving the brilliantly-lighted station the cars plunged into darkness, relieved by an occasional electric lamp.

"Must be a tunnel," thought Roy. "We'll come out on top of the ground in a minute, and I can see what New York looks like. Space is so crowded down town, I s'pose they have to tunnel for a few blocks."

But the tunnel did not come to an end. In vain Roy waited for the train to emerge into daylight. Past station after station it rushed, the lights there showing for an instant, and then the darkness closing in again.

Finally the express stopped. Several passengers got off, and more got on. Then it started up again, still whizzing through the dark.

Roy could stand it no longer. Perhaps he had made a mistake and gotten into the wrong train This one might be destined for China, or some other under-ground port. Roy made his way to where a guard was standing.

"Excuse me, stranger," he began, in his broad western tones. "But how long is this tunnel, anyhow?"

"Tunnel? This ain't no tunnel!"

"No? what is it then? It's a pretty good imitation. Looks like an underground river that has gone dry."

"Why, this is the subway."

"The subway?"

"Sure. It goes right under the streets, all the way along New York."

Then Roy understood. Mortimer De Royster had told him something of this underground railroad, through the heart of New York, but thinking of other things had put it out of Roy's mind. A little later he alighted and walked to his hotel.

Meanwhile Caleb Annister and Mr. Baker had been plotting together. They discussed many schemes, and at last hit on one they thought would answer.

"I think we'll let Tupper do the trick," said Baker. "Young Bradner saw less of him than he did of the rest of us, and if Tupper shaves off his moustache, and changes his voice a bit, as he can do, the boy will never recognize him," for

Baker had told Mr. Annister of the encounter of himself and his cronies with the boy from the ranch.

"Anything so as to get him away for two weeks," said the agent. "Don't tell him too much about it, and then—if anything happens, you understand—I can't be called to testify."

"Oh, nothing will happen, in the way you mean. We'll be careful. Now where is he stopping?"

Mr. Annister mentioned the name of the hotel, which Roy had written on the card he had left with the agent.

"All right. I'll see Tupper, and have him fix up to do the job. It ought to be easy. You'll have the money, I suppose?"

"As soon as he is out of the way—safely—you get the thousand dollars."

There was some more talk, and the two plotters separated.

It was three days after this, during which time Roy had enjoyed himself going about New York alone, (for he had not seen De Royster) that, as he was sitting in the hotel lobby one afternoon, a well-dressed man approached him.

"Aren't you from out Painted Stone way, in Colorado?" asked the man pleasantly.

"That's where I'm from, the Triple O ranch," replied Roy, who was frank by nature, and unsuspicious. He wondered who the man could be, and how he knew where he was from in the west.

"I thought so," went on the stranger. "I was out on a ranch

near there about a week ago and I happened to be at the railroad station when you got aboard."

"What ranch were you on?" asked Roy, for he knew them all within a radius of a hundred miles of his father's.

"Why, it was—er—let's see—seems to me it was the Double X."

"There's no such ranch near Painted Stone."

"Well, maybe I'm wrong. I just stopped there, but I have a poor memory for names," said the stranger quickly. "But permit me to introduce myself. I'm John Wakely, of Buffalo. I'm a stranger in New York, and, as you are also, I thought we might go about a bit together."

"That would suit me," replied Roy, who was beginning to feel a bit lonely in the big city, without the company of a friend. He thought this was a good opportunity to go around and see the sights. He told the man his name.

"Suppose we go in and have some ice cream soda," went on Mr. Wakely. "Or, better, still, have it in my room. I'm stopping at this hotel. Then we can go out a bit."

The idea appealed to Roy, who had a liking for the ice cream sodas he had only lately become familiar with. The day was hot, and the stranger seemed very cordial. Roy had a dim suspicion that he had heard his voice somewhere before, but he could not place it. Certainly the face was not one he could recall.

They went to Mr. Wakely's room, and soon a bell boy brought two large glasses of the cool beverage.

He set them down on the table between Mr. Wakely and Roy, and then withdrew. Had Roy known now of the dangers of the city he never would have trusted a stranger as he did this one.

"Is that your handkerchief on the floor behind you?" asked Mr. Wakely suddenly, pointing at something on the carpet.

Roy turned. At the same instant Mr. Wakely extended his hand over the glass of soda in front of the boy. Something like a white powder sifted down into it.

A moment later Roy turned back.

"It's not my handkerchief," he said. "Must be a piece of dust rag, the work-girl dropped."

"Very likely. But drink your soda and we'll go out." The boy put to his lips the glass, into which Mr. Wakely had sifted the white powder. He was in great danger, but he did not realize nor suspect it.

CHAPTER XIX

ROY IS MISSING

Shortly after this incident, approaching the clerk at the hotel desk where he had engaged a room near Roy's, Mr. Wakely, seeming much concerned, said:

"My friend, Mr. Bradner, has been taken suddenly ill. I think I shall take him to my doctor's. Will you call me a cab?"

"Why don't you have the hotel doctor look at him?" suggested the clerk, who had taken a liking to the boy from the ranch. The clerk did not exactly like the ways of Mr. Wakely, who had only taken a room at the hotel a day or so before.

"Oh, I don't like to trust a strange doctor. I think my physician can fix him up. He is in need of rest, more than anything else. The strenuous life of the city, after his quiet days on the ranch has been too much for him."

"He looked strong and hearty," replied the clerk. "He told me he used to rope wild steers. I should think he could stand it here. He hasn't been going around much."

"Still I think I shall take him away," went on Mr. Wakely.

"Please call me a cab. I believe I'll take his baggage with me. I'll settle for his bill."

"There's nothing to settle. Mr. Bradner paid me this morning for his board up to the end of the week."

Mr. Wakely looked relieved at this, but said nothing.

The clerk, not exactly liking what was going on, but being unable to interpose any objections, rung for a cab. Then, under orders from Mr. Wakely, Roy's baggage was brought down and put into the vehicle.

A little later Roy's new acquaintance came down in the elevator, supporting the lad with an arm around his shoulders. Roy could hardly walk, for his legs were trembling, and there was a curious white, dazed look on his face.

"What's the matter, old chap?" asked the hotel clerk, with ready sympathy. "Can I do anything for you?"

It seemed as if Roy tried to speak, but only a murmur came from his lips.

"He'll be all right in a little while," said Mr. Wakely quickly. "He's a little faint; that's all. I'll look after him."

Somehow the clerk thought Mr. Wakely acted as if he did not want any one to come too near Roy, or lend any aid. A little later, leading the boy, who seemed to become weaker, Mr. Wakely got into the cab with him, and drove on.

"Poor fellow," said the clerk sympathetically. "I hope he gets better. He certainly is a nice chap, and I wonder what could have made him ill so suddenly? I don't like that Wakely fellow."

That evening it occurred to Mortimer De Royster that he had not seen his friend Roy for some time. Not, in fact, since he had parted with him at the hotel.

"That's beastly impolite on my part, don't you know," said De Royster to himself. "I must run around and see him. I've been so busy straightening out my accounts since I came back from my western trip, that I have neglected all my friends. However, I'll make up for it. I'll take him to some theatre and give him a good time."

Thus musing, Mortimer De Royster adjusted his one eye glass, selected a delicately-colored necktie from his rather large stock, and attired himself to go out and call at Roy's hotel, which he soon reached.

"Good evening, Mortimer," greeted the clerk, who knew De Royster quite well. "How are you?"

"Feeling very fit, old chap, don't you know," replied De Royster. "How are you?"

"So-so."

"That's good. Charming evening, isn't it? Charming. I—er—I called to see my friend, Mr. Bradner. Going to take him out and show him a bit of New York after dark, don't you know. I have tickets to a very nice show, and I think he'll like it. I owe a good deal to him, old man. He's a clever chap. I want to repay him in some way. I'll go up to his room."

"It's no use."

"No use. Why, my dear fellow, what do you mean?"

"I mean he was taken away—ill—in a cab by a friend of his."

"Who was the friend?"

Mortimer De Royster lost his rather careless manner, and was all attention.

"A fellow named Wakely. He took rooms here a day or so ago. Made friends with Mr. Bradner—Roy, I call him, for I feel quite friendly toward him. Late this afternoon Wakely came to me and said Roy was sick, and he was going to take him to a doctor."

"And did he?"

"That's what he did. Took his baggage too," and the clerk related what had taken place.

"What sort of a fellow was this Wakely?" asked De Royster, with increasing interest.

The clerk described him. The dudish jewelry salesman shook his head.

"I don't recognize him," he said. "What do you think about it? You saw him."

"I'll tell you what I think," went on the clerk. "I think that fellow Wakely is up to some game, and I wish Roy had not made his acquaintance."

"That's just what I believe," exclaimed De Royster. "It seems a queer thing that Roy should be taken sick so suddenly. Why, he was as healthy as a young ox. I'll wager there's something wrong. He came here to New York to expose a man he thought was a swindler, and I believe the man has him in his power now. I must do something to aid him."

"What are you going to do?" asked the clerk, as De Royster started out of the hotel.

"I'm going to try to find the cab driver who took them away, and perhaps I can trace Roy. If I can't do it that way I'll notify the police. Roy has been taken away against his will, and maybe they are keeping him in hiding. I'm going to find him!"

Roused into sudden action by the thought of danger to the lad who had aided him, Mortimer De Royster hurried out, a look of determination on his face.

CHAPTER XX

IN THE TENEMENT

When Roy awakened, after what seemed like a very long sleep, he found himself in a poorly furnished room. At first he could not understand it—everything was so different from his pleasant apartment at the hotel.

He thought it must be a dream, but when he saw his trunk and valises near the bed, he knew he was not asleep.

He sat up and looked about him. The room he was in contained, besides the bed, a table, a few chairs and a small cupboard. As Roy roused a man, seated in one of the chairs, approached the bed.

"So, you're awake, are you?" he asked.

"What's the matter—what has happened, Mr. Wakely?" asked Roy, recognizing the man who had treated him to ice cream soda.

"Oh, you're all right. You're just staying here for a few days."

"But what happened? Did the hotel catch fire? Did I get hurt? Did they bring me here?"

Frank V. Webster

"I brought you here, but the hotel did not catch fire."

"Then why am I not there—in my own room?"

"This is your room for a while."

Something in the man's smile roused Roy's suspicions.

"What do you mean?" he asked quickly.

"Now keep quiet and you'll be all right," spoke Mr. Wakely, in what he meant to be a soothing tone. "You can't help yourself. You're here, and you're going to stay."

All of Roy's energies were aroused. He believed he had been brought to the place for the purposes of robbery. But how had it been done without his knowledge? He started to leave the bed.

"No you don't!" exclaimed Mr. Wakely. "You stay right there."

"What's that?" cried Roy, a sudden fire coming into his eyes, and his hands clenching themselves ready for a fray. "I must say you've got nerve to do this. I'm going to get up, and you and I are going to have a tussel! I guess I haven't roped wild steers, and ridden bucking broncos, for nothing!"

He threw off the covers, noting for the first time that he was fully dressed. But, as he attempted to approach Mr. Wakely a dizziness overcame him, and he sank back, trembling on the bed.

"You see I am right," went on the plotter with an evil smile. "You had better stay where you are."

It seemed to Roy as if all his strength had left him. He had never felt so weak before, save once, when he was recovering from a severe fever.

"Where am I; and what do you want?" he managed to ask.

"Now if you'll promise to lie quietly, I'll tell you," went on the man. "I guess I'll not take any chances though. I'll tie you in bed, and you can listen then."

It did not take him long, in Roy's weakened condition, to fasten the boy securely in the bed, by means of ropes which he took from the cupboard.

"There," remarked Mr. Wakely when he had finished. "I think you'll stay there for a while. Now listen. You have been brought here for a certain purpose. I can't tell you just what it is, but, if you behave yourself, no harm will come to you."

"But what right have you got to bring me here?"

"Never mind about that. You're here, and you're going to stay."

"I'll call for help, as soon as I'm able."

"And a lot of good it will do you. You are on the top floor of a tenement house, and there are no tenants except on the first floor. You can yell until you are hoarse, for there is a big electric light plant near here. It runs night and day and it makes so much noise constantly that all the yelling you can do won't be heard above it. Besides, if the tenants should happen to hear you yelling, they'll pay no attention to you, for you are supposed to be crazy. I told 'em so. Now you see how helpless you are."

Roy felt stunned. Why had this man gotten him in his power?

"But I can't see what you want of me," went on Roy weakly. "If it's money, why take what I have, if you mean to rob me."

"No. I'm not going to rob you."

"Then are you kidnapping me, and holding me for a ransom?" Roy had read of such things.

"Not much! Kidnapping isn't in my line. I am acting under orders for a friend of mine. He wants you kept out of the way for a while, and I'm going to do it.

"Now understand. I'm on guard here, or in the next room all the while. If I'm not there some one else will be. If you try to escape it will go hard with you. If you behave you'll be well taken care of, and fed. In a short time—that is, in a week or so—you will be allowed to go. Now, if you'll promise to lie quietly, I'll take off the ropes."

"I'll not promise you anything!"

"Very well, then you stay tied up. I'm going out for a few minutes, but you needn't think you can escape."

The man left, locking the door. As soon as he was gone Roy tried to loosen the bonds, but they were tied too tightly, and he was too weak to accomplish anything.

"I wonder what his object is?" thought the boy from the ranch. "He must have put some drug in that soda to make me partly unconscious. I remember now it had tasted queer. Then he brought me here. But what for? I can't understand it. I wonder if I can escape?"

Once more Roy tried to loosen the ropes, but the effort was too much, and his head, which was not tied down, fell back. He was unconscious.

Frank V. Webster

CHAPTER XXI

A DANGEROUS DESCENT

When Roy regained his senses again, he felt much better. He was still tied down on the bed, and Wakely was sitting near him.

"Well, you were quiet enough," remarked the man with a sneer. "I've got something here to eat. You can take it, if you don't raise a row."

"Oh, I'll take it," said Roy. He knew if he was to make an effort to escape, which he fully intended to do, he would need all his strength, and food was necessary.

"Then, I'll loosen the ropes a bit. But, mind now, no funny work, or I'll tackle you."

Roy had his own opinion as to how he would fare in a tussel with Wakely, but he said nothing. The ropes were loosened and the boy partook of the food. He felt better after it.

It was now dark, and Wakely lighted the gas in the room. Roy wondered whether it was the same day he had been taken from the hotel, or whether several had elapsed. It was the same day, as he learned later.

"Now, I'm going to sleep in the next room," went on the man, "and I warn you I'll awaken at the slightest sound. If you try any tricks—well, it will be better if you don't. As I said, no harm will come to you—if you're quiet."

Roy did not answer. He wanted to think out a plan of action. He was puzzled over the queer situation, and wondering who could have any object in keeping him a prisoner. He did not associate Caleb Annister with it.

After the meal Wakely again adjusted the ropes about the boy on the bed, and Roy offered no objections. He was sure when the time came he could undo the bonds. For what Roy did not know about tying ropes, to hold anything from a bucking bronco to a wild steer, was not worth knowing. He was in a situation now where his life on the ranch was likely to stand him in good stead.

"You can go to sleep whenever you want to," said Wakely. "But remember—no tricks!"

Roy did not answer. He wanted to think, and he knew he could do it best in the dark. Presently Wakely turned off the gas, and withdrew, again locking the door.

It did not need much listening on Roy's part to show that the man had spoken the truth about the noises near the tenement. There sounded the whirr of dynamos, the puffing of steam, the rattle of coal and ashes down chutes—in short it would have taken a loud voice to make itself heard above the racket. A better place to keep a prisoner, in the midst of a great city, could not have been devised.

Nevertheless Roy did not give up hope. He resolved to attempt nothing that night. He wanted daylight to work by, and he felt that Wakely could not be with him all the while.

"But if I stay here more than a day or so there's going to be trouble," thought the boy. "Dad will write or telegraph me, in answer to my letter telling about Annister's game, and, if I can't answer him, he'll get worried. I wish I could understand what this is all about. Maybe they take me for another person. Well, I can't do anything now. I must try to sleep. That stuff he gave me makes my head ache. This shows how foolish I was to trust too much to strangers. When he got me to look around at that handkerchief he must have put something into my soda."

Thus musing, Roy fell into a doze. From that he passed into a heavy sleep, and Wakely, peering in the door a little later, noted with satisfaction that his prisoner was deep in slumber.

"That's good," he whispered. "I can get some rest myself now. It's no joke—being on guard all the while. Some of the others of the gang have got to help out. I must send word to Baker. He's got to take his share."

Roy felt better the next morning, and ate with relish the breakfast Wakely brought in, though the meal was not a very good one.

A little while after this his captor went out, and Roy resolved to attempt to loosen his bonds. It was a hard task, for he could not work to advantage, but to his delight he found he could gradually undo some of the knots.

But he did not cast off the ropes. That was not his plan. As long as he knew he could loosen them at will, he decided to remain as though bound. This would make Wakely think he was in no position to escape, and the man would not keep such close watch.

Soon after this voices were heard in the outer room, and Roy knew some one was with his guard. They did not come into the apartment, and the boy saw nothing of any one until, at noon, more food was brought to him. He deemed it inadvisable to attempt to escape now, and resolved to wait another day.

Night came, supper was brought, and again Roy was locked in. He was beginning to be very uncomfortable, lying in bed so long.

"I'll slip out the first chance I get to-morrow," he thought. "Right after breakfast will be a good time."

Fortune favored him. Soon after Wakely had brought in the morning meal, he went out, locking the door after him. Roy heard another door close, and guessed rightly that his captor had left the building.

"Now's my chance!" thought the boy.

Putting into operation his knowledge of ropes and knots, and, by using his strength, which was not small, he managed to loosen his bonds. In a few minutes he was standing in the middle of the room free.

"Now for the door!" Roy murmured. "I wonder if I can break it open, or work the lock?"

A moment's inspection served to show him that to open the portal was out of the question. The lock was a heavy one. The door itself was solid, not one with panels, and, after trying it cautiously, for Roy did not want to make a noise, he decided he could not escape that way.

There was only one other means,—the window. He went to it and looked out. It was fully sixty feet from the ground, and there was nothing, in the shape of a lightning rod, or a rain-pipe leader to cling to. Nothing but the bare tenement house wall, broken here and there with other windows.

Roy leaned far out. He knew it was useless to shout, as the noise from the electric shop drowned all other sound. Nor could he see any one whose attention he might attract.

It was necessary for him that he work quickly, for Wakely, or one of his friends, might return any moment. Yet how could Roy get out of the window and to the ground?

He looked about the room for something to aid him. His first thought was of the bed clothes. He had read of persons tying sheets together, after tearing them into strips, and so making a rope. But there were no sheets on his bed, merely a small blanket, for it was warm weather. There was nothing in the shape of a rope in the room. It looked as if Roy would have to remain a prisoner.

Suddenly an idea came to him as he looked at his large valise which, with his trunk, had been brought to his room.

"I have it!" he exclaimed. "My lasso! It's long enough!"

It did not take a minute to get it from the valise. It was a long thin lariat, strong enough to support several pounds, and he knew it would reach over a hundred feet.

"Lucky I thought to bring that with me," he said, "though Billy Carew laughed at me, and asked if I expected to rope any steers in the streets of New York. I guess he didn't figure on this."

It did not take Roy two minutes to fasten one end of the lariat to the bed, which was the heaviest article in the room. Then he tossed the other end out of the window, noting that it touched the ground, with several feet to spare.

"Now for it!" murmured the boy. "It's a dangerous climb, to go down hand over hand, but I think I can slide it!"

Testing the lasso to make sure it was securely fastened, he put one leg over the window sill, grasped the lariat with both hands, and swung himself off.

As he did so he heard the door of his room open, and some one rushed in. There was a cry of alarm.

"That's Wakely," reasoned Roy. "He's discovered that I'm gone."

An instant later the face of Wakely appeared at the window. He shouted to Roy:

"Come back here!"

"Not much!"

"Then I'll cut the rope!"

Wakely drew out his knife, but, before he had a chance to use it he was pulled back, and the face of Mortimer De Royster replaced that of Roy's late captor.

CHAPTER XXII

GETTING A CLUE

Roy was so astonished at the sight of his friend, the jewelry salesman, peering out of the window that he nearly let go his hold of the rope. He recovered himself quickly, however, and slid on toward the ground. As he looked up at the casement he could see that De Royster and Wakely were having some kind of a struggle.

"I must go back and help him," thought Roy. "Mr. De Royster is no match for that fellow. I'd like to tackle him on my own account, though he was not cruel to me while he had me a prisoner."

His determination to do this was increased when his friend leaned out of the window, and called:

"Come on up, Roy! Help me!"

"He's plucky to tackle that fellow alone," thought the boy from the ranch.

But now he had no time for musings. He must act. As he let go the rope, his feet having touched the ground, he found himself in the not very clean yard of the tenement.

About him were boxes and barrels of rubbish, decaying vegetables were on all sides, besides tin cans and heaps of refuse. Clearly the tenants in the house were not particular.

Roy looked about him. The yard was surrounded by a high fence, and there were no persons in sight. To the rear was the electric light plant, and on either side, the yards of other tenement houses. Then Roy saw an alley, which, he thought, would lead to the street.

Leaving his lariat dangling, he made a dash for the alley and soon found himself in front of the tenement house, where he had so recently been a prisoner.

Up the stairs he went on the jump, and, as he came near the room where he had been held, he could hear the sound of a struggle.

"They're fighting!" he thought. "I must help De Royster!"

As he entered the apartment he saw the jewelry salesman holding Wakely by the wrists, while the man was endeavoring to get away.

"Quiet now, my dear fellow!" exclaimed Mortimer De Royster. "I say, old chap, you can't get away, don't you know. I've got you, and I'm going to have you arrested."

"You are, eh? I'll see about that!" exclaimed Wakely. "Let go of me!"

At the same time he gave a violent wrench.

"Hold on, my dear fellow," remonstrated De Royster. "You mustn't do that, don't you know."

In spite of his rather slight built De Royster was proving himself almost a match for Wakely. But his strength was not of the lasting kind, while the other's was.

"Let me go!" fiercely demanded Wakely. "If you don't it will be the worst for you!"

At the same time he gave such a yank that he succeeded in freeing one arm. But De Royster was not going to give up so easily. He grabbed Wakely around the waist.

At that moment Roy made a rush for Wakely. Just as he was about to grab him, he was thrust aside by some one from behind. Wakely turned, gave one look at the newcomer, and cried:

"Quick! Tell Annister he's escaped!"

Wakely had not yet observed Roy, as the boy from the ranch was back of him. Then the man who had taken Roy from the hotel succeeded in breaking the hold De Royster and Roy had on him. He dashed from the room, just as the other man, to whom he had called the warning, also ran out. Both seemed much frightened.

"Hold on!" cried De Royster, as if either of the men would stop for that. "Hold on! I know you."

"Come on! We'll get 'em!" shouted Roy, turning quickly and starting after his captor and the confederate.

But he was too late.

Wakely slammed the door of the room shut, and locked it, and Roy knew it would be useless to try and open it.

"Break the door down!" exclaimed Mortimer De Royster. "We can catch them!"

"The door's too strong," replied Roy.

"Then we're caught!"

"Yes, but don't worry. I can go down the lariat the same as I did before."

"Perhaps you can, but I can't my dear fellow."

"Oh, I'll come up the stairs and open the door for you, if the key's there. Say, but how did you get here, anyhow?"

"I came after you. I've been tracing you for hours. What does it all mean, Roy? Why did they take you a prisoner?"

"I don't know. Wait until I get my breath and I'll talk."

"That's so. I'm a little troubled that way myself, don't you know. If I could have held that chap a little longer I would have had him."

"Yes, but he had help at hand."

"Right again, old chap. The other man came in at the wrong time. You know who he was, don't you?"

"No. I didn't get a good look at his face. Who was he?"

"One of the four swindlers from out West who got my watch and diamond pin!"

"You don't mean it;" cried Roy, much excited. He began to understand part of the plot now.

"That's who he was," declared the dudish salesman. "I knew him at once, but I couldn't warn you. I needed all my breath to hold that other man. What was his name? I've forgotten."

"He called himself Wakely. I met him at my hotel."

The exciting incidents of the last few minutes, and the surprise created by De Royster's announcement that one of the train swindlers was a friend of Wakely, set Roy to thinking.

"Did you hear what the fellow, whom I was holding, said just before he got away?" asked Mr. De Royster, after a pause.

"Yes, he said 'Quick! Tell Annister he's escaped!'"

"I wonder what he meant?"

"I reckon I can explain. I might as well tell you the whole story of why I came to New York, and you will understand. Caleb Annister is the name of the man who is agent for some property my father and I own. It was this man whose actions I came to investigate. I found him to be a swindler, and I gave him a short time in which to pay back the money he had wrongfully retained."

"What did he say?"

"He tried to explain, but it was a pretty poor explanation. I caught him 'with the goods on him', as we say out West."

"But why should this man whom I held—this Wakely—want the other to warn Annister about some one escaping?"

"That 'some one' was me. I believe Annister got these fellows to get me out of the way for a time, until he could work some of his schemes. Perhaps he thought I would be frightened, and go back West, where I could not bother him any more.

"Are you going?"

"Not a bit. I'm going to keep right after him. I begin to see through his plot. This man Wakely came to my hotel purposely to get acquainted with me. Then he drugged me, and got me out to this place, where he kept me a prisoner. What was to be the outcome I don't know. But I am surprised to hear you say that the other man who came into the room was one of the swindlers who robbed you."

"I am sure of it. I would never forget his face. Wakely, too, seems familiar, but I can't place him."

"Maybe Wakely is a member of their gang, and perhaps Annister, too, is in with them."

"I shouldn't be surprised. What do you think we had better do?"

Neither of them yet recognized Wakely as Tupper.

"I think we'd better get out of this place before they come back with reinforcements," said Roy with a laugh. He was cool, despite what he had gone through, for he was somewhat used to meeting danger and doing his best to escape.

"I'll slide down my rope again," he went on, "come up the stairs, and open the door. Then we can talk it over. I must get my baggage away from here."

It did not take the boy long to repeat his feat with the lariat, and soon, having found a key, he opened the door from without, releasing Mortimer De Royster.

CHAPTER XXIII

A LAWYER'S ADVICE

"Now, what's the first thing to be done, my dear chap?" asked De Royster, as Roy loosed the lasso from the bed and coiled it up.

"Arrange to get my stuff away from here. I reckon, and back to my hotel. Then I want to hear how you traced me."

"I'll tell you. But I agree with you that we had better leave this place. Let's go down to the street and engage an expressman."

They found one who agreed to take Roy's baggage back to the hotel. After seeing it safely in the wagon, during which time a few of the tenants in the house looked on curiously, but said nothing, the two friends started for the hotel, where Roy had been stopping.

"As soon as I called at your hotel that night, and found you had been taken away, sick, by a man who had only recently come to the place, I suspected something was wrong," explained Mr. De Royster, on the way. "The clerk told me about you going away in a cab, and gave me a fairly good description of the driver, whom he had a glimpse of. It was a

Frank V. Webster

cab seldom seen in this part of the city.

"I knew my best plan, don't you know, would be to find that driver, and learn where he had taken you and your baggage. My idea was that some sharpers had gotten you into their power to rob you. I never suspected there was such a deep plot."

"Neither did I," replied Roy, "and I don't believe we have seen the last of it."

"Well," went on De Royster, "I had quite a time tracing that cabman. I must have interviewed nearly fifty drivers before I found one who knew a fellow that answered the description of the one who had taken you away. But at last I located him, and, though he was reluctant at first, to tell me what I wanted to know, he did, after I threatened to call in the police."

"Would you have done so?"

"Certainly. I felt that you were in danger, for you know little of New York."

"That's so, and I'm afraid it will take me a long time to learn. I'm pretty green."

"Well, you may be in some things, but you can go ahead of New Yorkers in lots of ways. That was a great trick, sliding down that lasso."

"It was lucky I had it with me."

"Indeed it was, and it was a good thing those scoundrels took your baggage as well as you, or you might have been there yet."

"No, for you would have helped me, I reckon. You arrived just a few minutes after I had started to escape. How did you manage it?"

"Well, as I said, my dear chap," replied De Royster, adjusting his one eye glass, which had fallen out during the struggle with Wakely, "I made the cabman tell me where he took you, and, after that it was an easy matter to locate you. I got to the tenement right behind Wakely and I followed him up the stairs, though, then, I didn't know who he was, and I rushed into the room as soon as he opened the door, for he forgot to close it when he looked at the bed and saw it empty. I suspected you had been in here, when I saw what a lonesome sort of place it was. I pulled him back, just as he had his knife out, ready to cut the lasso."

"I hardly believe he would have dared to cut it," said Roy. "He only wanted to scare me into coming back."

"Perhaps he did. But I was not going to take any chances; I just grabbed him."

"That was fine on your part."

"Oh, that's nothing. Look what you did for me. I only paid you back a little."

"Nonsense. As if I wanted pay."

"Of course you didn't, but I was glad of the chance. I only wish I could have held Wakely. Now, I suppose he'll go and tell Annister, and they'll keep right after you."

"Do you think so?"

"I believe so, from what you tell me of the men."

"Then what would you advise me to do?"

"Let me think it over a bit. Suppose we go to your room?"

"All right."

There was considerable surprise on the part of the clerk at the hotel when Roy came back. On the way he and Mortimer De Royster had agreed it would be better not to say anything about the reason for the taking away of the boy from the ranch—a veritable kidnapping in fact. So it was explained that Roy had recovered from his temporary illness, and had simply been away on business, which was true enough in its way,—though it was not very pleasant business.

"Now," said De Royster, when he and Roy were once more back in the former's room. "This is what I would do. I would consult a good lawyer, and let him advise me. I think this is too much for you to handle alone."

"I believe you are right. Do you know a good lawyer?"

"I can introduce you to the one who does business for our firm. He is very reliable, and his charges are reasonable."

"Then we will go see him, after I have changed my clothes. Sleeping in them hasn't made them look exactly as new as they were."

"That's a good idea. Have you heard from your father since writing to him about Annister?"

"I don't know. Perhaps a letter came while I was away. I wonder where they would send it?"

"They would keep it here until you gave them some

instructions for forwarding it. I'll inquire at the desk for you while you are changing your clothes."

As Roy had purchased two suits on coming to New York, he had a new one to put on, while the other was sent to be pressed. He had not finished dressing when De Royster came back.

"No letters, but there's a telegram," he said, handing Roy the yellow envelope.

The boy tore it open and read:

"Letter received. No doubt Annister is swindler. You are doing right. Keep after him. Don't spare expense. Take property from his control, and give to some good man. I leave it to you. Answer when you get this."

"Why this came yesterday," said Roy. "Dad will be wondering why he doesn't hear from me."

"Then you had better answer at once. There is a branch telegraph office in the hotel lobby. Write an answer and I'll take it down while you finish dressing."

A reply was soon prepared and sent. Meanwhile Roy got ready for the street and, accompanied by De Royster, he went to the lawyer's office.

The legal gentleman greeted Mortimer De Royster cordially. Roy was quite surprised to find out how many friends the jewelry salesman had. Everyone seemed to like him in spite of his odd ways.

Roy's story was soon told. The lawyer took off his gold spectacles, wiped them carefully with a silk handkerchief, replaced them, looked at Roy over the tops of them, and remarked:

"Hum!"

It was not very encouraging, nor did it tell very much. Roy began to fear he had not made himself clear.

"I would like—" he began.

"What you want is my advice as to how next to proceed; isn't it?" asked the lawyer, as though he had come to some decision, as indeed he had.

"Yes, sir."

"Well, I shall have to look into this matter of the property. Evidently Mr. Annister has some reason for wanting you out of the way. What it is we shall have to discover. Meanwhile you had better do nothing."

"But suppose they kidnap him again?" asked De Royster.

"I don't believe they'll dare do that. Perhaps you had better take care where you go, however. In the meanwhile I will make some inquiries about this property. I will communicate with you as soon as I have anything to report."

"Do you think you can make Mr. Annister give back the money he has wrongfully kept?" asked Roy.

"I'm afraid I can't give you an opinion until I have looked further into the case," said the lawyer with a smile. "It may be necessary to take civil action, and we might have to make a criminal complaint. Now don't worry about it. I'll look after it. Just you keep out of the way of those men."

"I will," agreed Roy with a laugh. "I'm not afraid of them, however. I'll be ready for them next time."

"Another thing," went on the lawyer, "don't drink ice cream sodas, or anything else, with strangers."

"I'll stick to Mr. De Royster," said the boy. "I reckon if I trail along with him they'll not be able to rope me."

"Rope you? Oh, yes, I understand," replied the lawyer with a smile. "Yes, that's right. Good morning."

Frank V. Webster

CHAPTER XXIV

ANOTHER RASCALLY ATTEMPT

"What next?" asked Roy of Mortimer De Royster, as they emerged from the lawyer's office.

"Well, as it's getting near dinner time, suppose we go back to the hotel."

"That's a good idea. Will you stay and have grub with me—I mean lunch. I must get used to calling it that while I'm in New York."

"Yes, thank you. I've got a good appetite since that tussel with Wakely."

"You had nerve to tackle him."

"I thought he was going to cut the rope and let you drop."

"If he had, that would have been the end of me. I'd have 'passed in my chips,' as the card players say."

"Those card players! I'd like to meet them. I'd get even with them for stealing my watch and diamond!"

"Maybe you'll have a chance, when we round up Annister."

"If we ever do. But I imagine he's too slick a criminal to be caught."

"We'll see," said Roy.

"What would you like to do this afternoon?" asked De Royster, when the meal was finished. "I can show you some sights if you'd like to see them."

"I sure would. I haven't had much time so far. There wasn't a great deal to see in that tenement."

"Then we'll go up to Bronx Park. We can make a quick trip in the subway."

"That's the place I thought was a tunnel, and I was wondering when we would come to the end," and Roy laughed at the memory of his natural mistake.

The two friends had a good time in the Park, looking at the animals. The herd of buffalo interested Roy very much, as did the elephants, tigers, and other beasts from tropical countries, for he had never seen any before, since no circuses ever came to Painted Stone, nor anywhere in that vicinity.

"You haven't got any of these out West; have you?" asked Mortimer De Royster, with a New Yorker's usual pride in the big Zoo.

"No, and we don't want 'em."

"Why not?"

"They'd stampede the cattle in seven counties. What would a drove of steers or a band of horses do if they saw one of them elephants coming at 'em, so's they couldn't tell which end was the tail? Or one of them long-necked giraffes? Why, those giraffes would starve out our way. There's no trees tall enough for 'em to eat their breakfast from."

They went into the reptile house, and the snakes fascinated Roy. He paused before a glass box of rattlers.

"There's something we've got out West," he said, "and we'd give a good deal not to have 'em. We lose lots of cattle from snake-bites—those ugly rattlers! I don't like to look at 'em! I nearly stepped on one once, and he stuck his fangs in my boot."

"What did you do?"

"Stepped on it and killed it. Come on; let's look at something more pleasant."

They spent the rest of the day in the Park, and returned to the hotel that evening.

For about a week nothing occurred. Mortimer De Royster took Roy for occasional pleasure trips, including one jaunt to Coney Island, where the boy from the ranch had his first glimpse of the ocean. The big waves, and the immense expanse of water, astonished him more than anything he had seen in New York.

"I never knew there was so much water in the world," he said. "This would be fine out our way in time of drouth, when all the pastures dry up."

"I'm afraid it would be worse than none at all," said Mr. De Royster. "It's salt, and it would kill the grass."

"That's so. I didn't think about that."

They went in bathing, and took in many amusements at the pleasure resort. It was quite late when they got back to the hotel, and De Royster did not go all the way with Roy, turning off to go to his own boarding house, which was about a mile from where Roy was stopping.

"I'll see you to-morrow," called the jewelry salesman, as the two parted. "I guess the lawyer will have some word for us then."

"There's a note for you," said the hotel clerk to Roy as the boy entered, and he handed over a sealed envelope. In the upper left hand corner was the printed name and address of the lawyer to whom De Royster had taken him.

"Mr. Felix Ketchum must have some news for me," thought Roy, as he opened the note. It was a written request for him to call at a certain address that night, where he would receive some information that would be of service to him, and the communication was signed with Mr. Ketchum's name. A postscript stated that the lawyer would be there.

"That's queer," thought the boy. "I wonder why he didn't have me call at his office? But perhaps he has to work secretly against Annister. I guess that's it."

"When did this note come?" he asked the clerk.

"Right after dinner."

"Dinner?"

"I mean the evening dinner—I suppose you call it supper out West," and the clerk smiled.

"That's what we do. Who brought this?"

"A boy. He said there was no answer. Hope it isn't bad news."

"No; only a business matter. Can you tell me where the Bowery is?"

"The Bowery. You're not going there; are you?"

"Yes, I have an appointment to meet a man there," and Roy mentioned the number.

"You want to be careful," cautioned the clerk. "It's not the best place in the world after dark. Don't take much money with you, for you might be robbed."

"Aren't there policemen there?"

"Yes, but they can't be all over. That address is not far from the Chinese district, and it's a hanging-out place for thieves and criminals."

"Funny that Mr. Ketchum should want me to go there," thought Roy, "but perhaps he has to get evidence against Mr. Annister from a man who doesn't care to be seen during the day. I guess I'll chance it. There can't be much danger in the midst of a big city, with policemen around. Besides I'll be on my guard. I wish I could tell Mr. De Royster. But, no, I'll not bother him. He'll think I'm a regular baby, not able to take care of myself."

This thought decided Roy to go alone. He suspected nothing, but, had he known more about New York, he would have considered twice before venturing into one of the worst parts of that great city.

The clerk once more cautioned the boy, gave him directions how to get to the address on the Bowery, and in due time Roy arrived there. Part of the street was brilliantly lighted, but the building where he was directed to call, was in a dark location, and did not look very inviting.

"I wonder if this is it?" thought Roy. "Guess I'll ask."

He saw a door opening into a dim hallway. A man was standing there.

"Is Mr. Ketchum in this building?" asked Roy, for the note had instructed him to ask for the lawyer.

"Yes, come on in," said the man gruffly.

Roy advanced. The door shut after him with a click, and he was left in almost total darkness. At the same time he felt some one grab him.

"Have you got him?" cried a voice. "Don't hurt him, but hold him tight."

Roy recognized the voice as that of Caleb Annister!

As he felt arms closing around him he kicked out vigorously. There was a howl of pain, but Roy was not released. He knew that once more he was in the hands of Annister's accomplices.

Frank V. Webster

CHAPTER XXV

THE ROUND-UP—CONCLUSION

Across Roy's mind it flashed in an instant that he had been deceived by the note—it was a forgery. He had been tricked into coming to the Bowery. He dwelt but momentarily on this, however, for he needed to devote all his attention to escaping from the grip of the man who held him.

Fortunately Roy was of exceptional strength for so young a lad. His training on the ranch, roping steers, training wild horses, and his life in the open, made him more than a match for the average man.

He kicked out vigorously, right and left, and squirmed like an eel. He felt the grip of the man relaxing, and heard him call for aid. Then another came.

But Roy was fighting desperately. He made up his mind not only not to let the men take him away again, but to hold them until help came. With this in view he set up a loud shout.

"Police! Police! Police!" he cried, remembering what the hotel clerk had said about the bluecoats being on the Bowery.

"Stop his mouth or we'll all be arrested!" exclaimed some one.

"Yes. Can't you manage him?" asked Annister desperately.

"He's as strong as a horse!" Roy heard one man grunt, and this caused the boy to smile grimly.

The struggle in the dark continued. The boy had a good grip on two men, and was preventing them from dragging him down the dark hallway.

But help was at hand. His cries had been heard in the street, and, a moment later the door leading to the thoroughfare opened, and a little light came in.

At the same time Roy heard the sound of a club striking on the pavement.

"The cops are coming!" cried a voice.

A few seconds later a burly bluecoat entered the door.

"What's going on?" he asked.

"Nothing but a drunken row," quickly replied one of the men who had attacked Roy, at the same time trying to loosen the grip of the lad. "I'm putting the fellow out."

The plotter would have been glad to drop the matter now and escape, but Roy had no intention of letting him go.

"Officer!" exclaimed Roy quickly, "they're trying to get me away! I've got hold of two of 'em. Give us a hand and we'll throw and tie 'em both."

He talked as though he was on the ranch, handling a pair of refractory calves.

Somehow the officer recognized the honesty in Roy's voice. He knew it was not uncommon for thieves and pickpockets to attack persons in dark hallways. He supposed it was one of those cases.

"I'll help you!" he exclaimed, quickly advancing. Some one in the rear of the hall had opened a door, and the place was lighter. The policeman saw two men whom Roy had gripped, holding them by twisting his hands in their coats. The men tried to escape.

"No, you don't!" exclaimed the officer, grabbing one. "I've got you."

At the same time a second policeman appeared, and took charge of the other. The rest of the men escaped.

"Now let's see who we've got," said the first bluecoat, as he led his prisoner to the light in the rear. His brother officer did likewise.

"I don't know either of 'em," announced the first policeman.

"Me either," admitted his colleague. "They must belong to a new pickpocket gang."

But Roy knew them both. One was Caleb Annister, and the other John Wakely, alias Dennison Tupper, though Roy did not learn that until later.

"Do you want to make a charge against these two?" asked the first officer. "A charge of attempted pocket picking?"

"It's worse than that," replied Roy. "They tried to kidnap me."

"Kidnap you? Then you'd better come to the station, and tell the sergeant all about it. I'll ring for the wagon."

In a little while the patrol vehicle dashed up with a clanging of the gong, and, through the great crowd that almost instantly gathered, Roy followed the two officers and their prisoners into the wagon. They were soon at the station house.

"How do I know but what you're all of one gang?" asked the sergeant, when Roy had told his story, while the other two remained obstinately silent.

"If you will telephone for Mr. Ketchum he will identify me."

The name produced an instant effect, for Mr. Ketchum was a lawyer well known in police circles, as he prosecuted many criminals.

The sergeant telephoned, and, in a short time, came the answer from Mr. Ketchum's home that he would come to the station and identify Roy.

He did so, and the sergeant admitted his mistake.

"I'll just lock these two up," he said, indicating Mr. Annister and Wakely.

"You're not going to lock me up, are you?" asked Caleb Annister, who seemed to lose all courage as he saw the way matters were going. "You're not going to prosecute me, are you, Roy Bradner? I'll make restitution! I'll pay it all back!"

"Then you confess you swindled this boy, and his father?" asked Mr. Ketchum quickly.

"I—er—I won't say anything," replied the other sullenly, as he saw the mistake he had made.

"You don't have to. I have evidence enough to convict you without any admissions on your part. I discovered your scheme in time. A few days more and it would have been too late to pay the taxes, and save the property for Mr. Bradner and his son."

"Was he going to take the property?" asked Roy, amazed at the duplicity of the agent his father had trusted.

"He was. That is why he tried to have you put out of the way. He was afraid you would interfere with his plan before the two weeks expired. Fortunately I discovered it in time. To-morrow I will pay the taxes in your father's name, and the building will remain the property of him and yourself."

"What's the charge against these two, then?" asked the sergeant.

"Attempted kidnapping and embezzlement against him," replied Mr. Ketchum, indicating Annister, "and against Wakely, a charge of actual kidnapping. I think we shall be able to arrest the others in the gang, also."

"Hold on!" exclaimed a voice, and Roy turned around to behold Mortimer De Royster. "There's another charge to be made."

"Who against?" asked the sergeant, impressed by the apparently wealthy air of the jewelry salesman.

"Against him," pointing to Wakely.

"What is the charge?"

"Robbery. He and three others stole my gold watch and diamond pin."

Wakely uttered an exclamation.

"I now recognize him as one of the robbers, even though he has shaved his moustache off," went on De Royster, and Roy, now, also knew where it was he had heard Wakely's voice before.

"Lock 'em up!" called the sergeant to the doorman, as he made an entry on the blotter, against the prisoners' names. "You can see the Judge in the morning," he went on. "I suppose you will be here, Mr. Ketchum?"

"Oh, yes. I will prosecute this case to a finish. It was a wicked and bold attempt at swindling."

"Well, you seem to turn up every time I need you," remarked Roy to Mortimer De Royster. "How did you know I was here?"

"I called at your hotel shortly after you left. I had forgotten to tell you, when we parted, that I would call for you early to-morrow morning. The clerk said you had gone to the Bowery, after receiving a note.

"I was suspicious, and I followed. I got there just as the patrol wagon left, and I came on to the station house. Well, I guess you 'rounded them up' as you call it, Roy."

"Yes, they're roped and in the corral now, all right. That is, part of them are."

"The police will get the others. They'll make Annister and Wakely tell who their confederates are."

Mortimer De Royster's surmise proved correct. Later that night Hynard, Baker and Sutton were arrested, just as they were about to leave the city. On Sutton were found pawn tickets representing De Royster's watch and diamond, and he got them back in due time. There were also some envelopes and letter heads secured in some criminal way from Mr. Ketchum's office. On one of them the note to Roy had been written.

After a hearing the swindlers and Annister, the rascally real estate agent, were sent to jail, in default of bail, there to await trial on several charges.

Eventually they were sent to prison for long terms.

"Well, you saved your father's building for him," remarked Mr. Ketchum to Roy, a few days later.

"Do you really think Annister could have gotten it into his possession?"

"He could, under the law. Of course we might have contested it, but it would have been a long and expensive proceeding. He would have had a tax deed to it, and that is considered pretty good. Your father can be proud of you. What are you going to do now?"

"Go back to the ranch, I guess. I've done all dad told me to, except get a good man to look after the property. Perhaps you can suggest some one?"

"I think I can arrange that without difficulty."

"Then I wish you would. I know my father would be glad to have you."

This was done a few days later, and Mr. Bradner was informed, by telegraph, of what had transpired. He could now be sure of getting all the rent money from the Bleeker Building. Little was ever recovered of the money that Mr. Annister had unlawfully retained, for his property was so tied up that the law could not touch it.

"Now, since your business is all attended to, why can't you stay in New York a few weeks longer, and see more of the sights?" proposed Mortimer De Royster to the boy from the ranch.

"I think I will," decided Roy.

"Besides, you have still a visit to make."

"A visit?"

"Exactly. You must call on that lady of the runaway."

"Oh! I reckon she has forgotten me," answered the boy from the ranch.

But he had not been forgotten, as a visit to the lady's home quickly proved. He was royally entertained, and the lady's husband insisted upon presenting him with a ruby scarf pin, doing so in the names of both his wife and his little daughter.

"And now you've got to make me a promise," said Roy to Mortimer De Royster, when the boy from the ranch was ready to go home.

"All right, Roy, anything you say goes."

"You must visit our ranch soon. I'll show you the best time possible."

"I don't know what sort of a figure I'd cut on a ranch," answered the jewelry salesman, with a faint smile. "Don't forget how I got mixed up with those sharpers when I was out in your neighborhood."

"We haven't any sharpers at our ranch. If they came around where we were our cowboys would treat them pretty rough, I can tell you that. I'd like to get you on one of our ponies and ride you across the ranges. You'd find it the best kind of outdoor exercise."

"I believe you there, Roy."

"Then you will come? I want you to meet my father. You'll soon get used to our style of living—just as I got used to city ways." And the boy from the ranch grinned as he thought of the experiences he had undergone.

"I'll come if I possibly can," answered Mortimer De Royster. Let me add here that he did come, during the following July, and he and Roy had many a good time together, hunting, fishing, and rounding-up cattle.

It must be admitted that Roy was anxious to get home, to see his father and tell his parent the details of what had transpired. He found his father much improved, for which he was thankful.

"Roy, you did well—as well as any man could have done," said Mr. Bradner. "I am proud of you." And his beaming face showed he meant what he said.

It was a happy reunion. The cowboys were also glad to have the boy among them again, and that night they held a sort of jollification, lighting a big bonfire and shooting off their firearms as if it was the Fourth of July. And here let us take our leave of The Boy from the Ranch.

Choose from Thousands of 1stWorldLibrary Classics By

A. M. Barnard
Ada Leverson
Adolphus William Ward
Aesop
Agatha Christie
Alexander Aaronsohn
Alexander Kielland
Alexandre Dumas
Alfred Gatty
Alfred Ollivant
Alice Duer Miller
Alice Turner Curtis
Alice Dunbar
Allen Chapman
Alleyne Ireland
Ambrose Bierce
Amelia E. Barr
Amory H. Bradford
Andrew Lang
Andrew McFarland Davis
Andy Adams
Angela Brazil
Anna Alice Chapin
Anna Sewell
Annie Besant
Annie Hamilton Donnell
Annie Payson Call
Annie Roe Carr
Annonaymous
Anton Chekhov
Archibald Lee Fletcher
Arnold Bennett
Arthur C. Benson
Arthur Conan Doyle
Arthur M. Winfield
Arthur Ransome
Arthur Schnitzler
Arthur Train
Atticus
B.H. Baden-Powell
B. M. Bower
B. C. Chatterjee
Baroness Emmuska Orczy
Baroness Orczy
Basil King
Bayard Taylor
Ben Macomber
Bertha Muzzy Bower
Bjornstjerne Bjornson

Booth Tarkington
Boyd Cable
Bram Stoker
C. Collodi
C. E. Orr
C. M. Ingleby
Carolyn Wells
Catherine Parr Traill
Charles A. Eastman
Charles Amory Beach
Charles Dickens
Charles Dudley Warner
Charles Farrar Browne
Charles Ives
Charles Kingsley
Charles Klein
Charles Hanson Towne
Charles Lathrop Pack
Charles Romyn Dake
Charles Whibley
Charles Willing Beale
Charlotte M. Braeme
Charlotte M. Yonge
Charlotte Perkins Stetson
Clair W. Hayes
Clarence Day Jr.
Clarence E. Mulford
Clemence Housman
Confucius
Coningsby Dawson
Cornelis DeWitt Wilcox
Cyril Burleigh
D. H. Lawrence
Daniel Defoe
David Garnett
Dinah Craik
Don Carlos Janes
Donald Keyhoe
Dorothy Kilner
Dougan Clark
Douglas Fairbanks
E. Nesbit
E. P. Roe
E. Phillips Oppenheim
E. S. Brooks
Earl Barnes
Edgar Rice Burroughs
Edith Van Dyne
Edith Wharton

Edward Everett Hale
Edward J. O'Biren
Edward S. Ellis
Edwin L. Arnold
Eleanor Atkins
Eleanor Hallowell Abbott
Eliot Gregory
Elizabeth Gaskell
Elizabeth McCracken
Elizabeth Von Arnim
Ellem Key
Emerson Hough
Emilie F. Carlen
Emily Bronte
Emily Dickinson
Enid Bagnold
Enilor Macartney Lane
Erasmus W. Jones
Ernie Howard Pie
Ethel May Dell
Ethel Turner
Ethel Watts Mumford
Eugene Sue
Eugenie Foa
Eugene Wood
Eustace Hale Ball
Evelyn Everett-green
Everard Cotes
F. H. Cheley
F. J. Cross
F. Marion Crawford
Fannie E. Newberry
Federick Austin Ogg
Ferdinand Ossendowski
Fergus Hume
Florence A. Kilpatrick
Fremont B. Deering
Francis Bacon
Francis Darwin
Frances Hodgson Burnett
Frances Parkinson Keyes
Frank Gee Patchin
Frank Harris
Frank Jewett Mather
Frank L. Packard
Frank V. Webster
Frederic Stewart Isham
Frederick Trevor Hill
Frederick Winslow Taylor

Friedrich Kerst	Hayden Carruth	James Branch Cabell
Friedrich Nietzsche	Helent Hunt Jackson	James DeMille
Fyodor Dostoyevsky	Helen Nicolay	James Joyce
G.A. Henty	Hendrik Conscience	James Lane Allen
G.K. Chesterton	Hendy David Thoreau	James Lane Allen
Gabrielle E. Jackson	Henri Barbusse	James Oliver Curwood
Garrett P. Serviss	Henrik Ibsen	James Oppenheim
Gaston Leroux	Henry Adams	James Otis
George A. Warren	Henry Ford	James R. Driscoll
George Ade	Henry Frost	Jane Abbott
Geroge Bernard Shaw	Henry James	Jane Austen
George Cary Eggleston	Henry Jones Ford	Jane L. Stewart
George Durston	Henry Seton Merriman	Janet Aldridge
George Ebers	Henry W Longfellow	Jens Peter Jacobsen
George Eliot	Herbert A. Giles	Jerome K. Jerome
George Gissing	Herbert Carter	Jessie Graham Flower
George MacDonald	Herbert N. Casson	John Buchan
George Meredith	Herman Hesse	John Burroughs
George Orwell	Hildegard G. Frey	John Cournos
George Sylvester Viereck	Homer	John F. Kennedy
George Tucker	Honore De Balzac	John Gay
George W. Cable	Horace B. Day	John Glasworthy
George Wharton James	Horace Walpole	John Habberton
Gertrude Atherton	Horatio Alger Jr.	John Joy Bell
Gordon Casserly	Howard Pyle	John Kendrick Bangs
Grace E. King	Howard R. Garis	John Milton
Grace Gallatin	Hugh Lofting	John Philip Sousa
Grace Greenwood	Hugh Walpole	John Taintor Foote
Grant Allen	Humphry Ward	Jonas Lauritz Idemil Lie
Guillermo A. Sherwell	Ian Maclaren	Jonathan Swift
Gulielma Zollinger	Inez Haynes Gillmore	Joseph A. Altsheler
Gustav Flaubert	Irving Bacheller	Joseph Carey
H. A. Cody	Isabel Cecilia Williams	Joseph Conrad
H. B. Irving	Isabel Hornibrook	Joseph E. Badger Jr
H.C. Bailey	Israel Abrahams	Joseph Hergesheimer
H. G. Wells	Ivan Turgenev	Joseph Jacobs
H. H. Munro	J.G.Austin	Jules Vernes
H. Irving Hancock	J. Henri Fabre	Julian Hawthrone
H. R. Naylor	J. M. Barrie	Julie A Lippmann
H. Rider Haggard	J. M. Walsh	Justin Huntly McCarthy
H. W. C. Davis	J. Macdonald Oxley	Kakuzo Okakura
Haldeman Julius	J. R. Miller	Karle Wilson Baker
Hall Caine	J. S. Fletcher	Kate Chopin
Hamilton Wright Mabie	J. S. Knowles	Kenneth Grahame
Hans Christian Andersen	J. Storer Clouston	Kenneth McGaffey
Harold Avery	J. W. Duffield	Kate Langley Bosher
Harold McGrath	Jack London	Kate Langley Bosher
Harriet Beecher Stowe	Jacob Abbott	Katherine Cecil Thurston
Harry Castlemon	James Allen	Katherine Stokes
Harry Coghill	James Andrews	L. A. Abbot
Harry Houidini	James Baldwin	L. T. Meade

L. Frank Baum	Owen Johnson	Stephen Crane
Latta Griswold	P.G. Wodehouse	Stewart Edward White
Laura Dent Crane	Paul and Mabel Thorne	Stijn Streuvels
Laura Lee Hope	Paul G. Tomlinson	Swami Abhedananda
Laurence Housman	Paul Severing	Swami Parmananda
Lawrence Beasley	Percy Brebner	T. S. Ackland
Leo Tolstoy	Percy Keese Fitzhugh	T. S. Arthur
Leonid Andreyev	Peter B. Kyne	The Princess Der Ling
Lewis Carroll	Plato	Thomas A. Janvier
Lewis Sperry Chafer	Quincy Allen	Thomas A Kempis
Lilian Bell	R. Derby Holmes	Thomas Anderton
Lloyd Osbourne	R. L. Stevenson	Thomas Bailey Aldrich
Louis Hughes	R. S. Ball	Thomas Bulfinch
Louis Joseph Vance	Rabindranath Tagore	Thomas De Quincey
Louis Tracy	Rahul Alvares	Thomas Dixon
Louisa May Alcott	Ralph Bonehill	Thomas H. Huxley
Lucy Fitch Perkins	Ralph Henry Barbour	Thomas Hardy
Lucy Maud Montgomery	Ralph Victor	Thomas More
Luther Benson	Ralph Waldo Emmerson	Thornton W. Burgess
Lydia Miller Middleton	Rene Descartes	U. S. Grant
Lyndon Orr	Ray Cummings	Upton Sinclair
M. Corvus	Rex Beach	Valentine Williams
M. H. Adams	Rex E. Beach	Various Authors
Margaret E. Sangster	Richard Harding Davis	Vaughan Kester
Margret Howth	Richard Jefferies	Victor Appleton
Margaret Vandercook	Richard Le Gallienne	Victor G. Durham
Margaret W. Hungerford	Robert Barr	Victoria Cross
Margret Penrose	Robert Frost	Virginia Woolf
Maria Edgeworth	Robert Gordon Anderson	Wadsworth Camp
Maria Thompson Daviess	Robert L. Drake	Walter Camp
Mariano Azuela	Robert Lansing	Walter Scott
Marion Polk Angellotti	Robert Lynd	Washington Irving
Mark Overton	Robert Michael Ballantyne	Wilbur Lawton
Mark Twain	Robert W. Chambers	Wilkie Collins
Mary Austin	Rosa Nouchette Carey	Willa Cather
Mary Catherine Crowley	Rudyard Kipling	Willard F. Baker
Mary Cole	Saint Augustine	William Dean Howells
Mary Hastings Bradley	Samuel B. Allison	William le Queux
Mary Roberts Rinehart	Samuel Hopkins Adams	W. Makepeace Thackeray
Mary Rowlandson	Sarah Bernhardt	William W. Walter
M. Wollstonecraft Shelley	Sarah C. Hallowell	William Shakespeare
Maud Lindsay	Selma Lagerlof	Winston Churchill
Max Beerbohm	Sherwood Anderson	Yei Theodora Ozaki
Myra Kelly	Sigmund Freud	Yogi Ramacharaka
Nathaniel Hawthrone	Standish O'Grady	Young E. Allison
Nicolo Machiavelli	Stanley Weyman	Zane Grey
O. F. Walton	Stella Benson	
Oscar Wilde	Stella M. Francis